ADRIFT

ADRIFT

A Secret Life of
London's Waterways

Helen Babbs

ICON

Published in the UK in 2016 by
Icon Books Ltd, Omnibus Business Centre,
39–41 North Road, London N7 9DP
email: info@iconbooks.com
www.iconbooks.com

Sold in the UK, Europe and Asia
by Faber & Faber Ltd, Bloomsbury House,
74–77 Great Russell Street,
London WC1B 3DA or their agents

Distributed in the UK, Europe and Asia
by TBS Ltd, TBS Distribution Centre, Colchester Road,
Frating Green, Colchester CO7 7DW

Distributed in the USA
by Publishers Group West,
1700 Fourth Street, Berkeley, CA 94710

Distributed in Australia and New Zealand
by Allen & Unwin Pty Ltd,
PO Box 8500, 83 Alexander Street,
Crows Nest, NSW 2065

Distributed in South Africa
by Jonathan Ball, Office B4, The District,
41 Sir Lowry Road, Woodstock 7925

Distributed in Canada
by Publishers Group Canada,
76 Stafford Street, Unit 300
Toronto, Ontario M6J 2S1

ISBN: 978-184831-920-2

Typeset in Proforma by Marie Doherty

Printed and bound in the UK
by Clays Ltd, St Ives plc

Contents

winter, marshland
1. storm   5
2. boat   7
3. fen   27
4. river   39
5. unreal city   51

spring, wasteland
6. the cut   79
7. flora, fauna   91
8. homecoming   113
9. rites   123
10. fragments   139

summer, heartland
11. lost ways   157
12. truth, illusion   185
13. outside edges   201

autumn, metroland
14. voyage out   231
15. underbelly   243
16. adrift   253

Endnotes   277
Bibliography   289
Acknowledgements   295

winter

— ◆ —

marshland

River Lea and Lee Navigation
Leyton Marsh to Limehouse

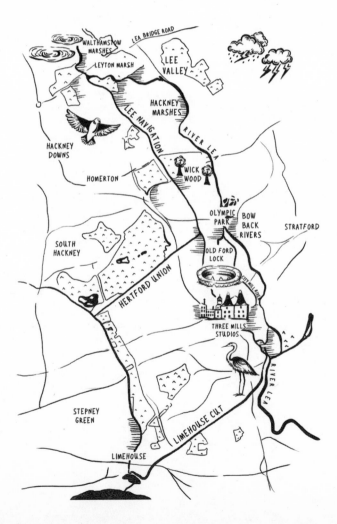

1. storm

It's dark out. In here it's warm and orange-lit, flickering. The smell is wet coal and woodsmoke. The sound, violent: high-pitched whistles and metallic cracks. The boat shifts and shudders, moans and rolls, more like a ship at sea than a broad barge on a narrow river. Dislocated branches suck across the Lea at speed, dragging their claws over the roof before rushing mad into the marshes. Suddenly there's a smash and scraping overhead as the wind grabs hold of the chimney's rain hat, rips it off and carries it, bouncing, away. The fire shudders in the stove, spits and starts, then settles again into its gentle, giving roar. Sometimes it's possible to forget this is a home without bricks, that she floats free of foundations. Not tonight. Tonight she is a tin drum, beaten by a thousand furious drumsticks. Tonight she is the weather's toy, to toss and whip at will.

It has poured and blown like this for weeks and weeks, and the world is taking on an underwater aspect. Christmas has been and gone in a tumult. Stowed away against the terrible storms, we've spent the holidays drinking whisky and watching trashy box set television on a tiny laptop. A gaudy noble fir, decked to disappearing in tinsel, slow cooks in the corner beside the red-hot stove. Our existence has shrunk itself into a few woozy square feet. We need to get out.

Next morning, when daylight cracks weak and grey, we dress from head to toe in waterproofs and wellies and air ourselves on the marshes. Water pools on top of the grass and starts to form streams. A moorhen has swapped river for sodden ground and busies itself in a swollen puddle. Leviathans gather on the horizon, promising more storm to come. We pretend they hide mountains. And we walk, bent against the weather, in a slow, looping ellipse, the boat never far from view. Dog walkers follow similar circles. Slapped cheeks flood with colour, cold eyes prick with tears, fur spikes. In a moment of abandon we let our hoods drop and allow the wet wind to catch our hair.

2. boat

It's early January and we're moored on the peripheries of the city, where Leyton Marsh meets Walthamstow Marsh, just downriver from Springfield. The storms that have wracked the country for most of the winter are easing off but the mud remains. London feels swamp-like, primaeval. Dickens's megalosaurus will surely be seen wandering across the marshes at any moment. The boat is brown-streaked and bramble-scratched. Lying in bed with my boyfriend S., we search for the willpower to get up, each urging the other to make a decisive first move. We blow breath rings, listening to a chorus of creaking rope and fender, the Lea's particular slap and gurgle, and a crow's serrating caws. A boat passes close by. We don't see it but we feel it as we slide forward, back, side to side in its wake. Condensation drips from the brass mushroom vent above us and leaves an accusing dark mark on the covers.

It's been a hard night. We got in late and didn't light a fire, cockily didn't even fill a hot water bottle. We thought single malt was enough and resolved to brush our teeth in our coats. We have been punished. The cold crept in in the small hours, seeping through the floorboards and under the doors. It was so penetrating it woke us up. A crystalline presence in the room that seized at every limb. Slipping in and out of sleep, I imagined my soft organs icing over, my bones splintering into jagged pieces of ice. Sunrise brought some relief and the space between the sheets slowly warmed, but the heat feels hard won and difficult to give up.

The cabin is properly insulated – and has a fairly successful attempt at double glazing in some rooms, if you will allow industrial-strength cling film to stand in for a secondary sheet of glass – but there's no escaping the fact that our home is made from steel and that that steel is partly submerged in a cold body of water. When standing up inside, the area below the knee is technically underwater. Unless the fire is lit, the temperature inside the boat can easily drop below freezing. That period of indefinite length between getting up and the cabin warming up is an unpleasant one to step into, so we continue to hunker, to extend the conversation that keeps us in bed. These days, we tell each other, it's an effort to remember how it felt to wake up on dry land, how it felt to live in the same street, the same borough, for months, maybe years on end. We course through London, following her navigable waterways, cruising ever onwards. There's always another local to drink in and so many different corners with so many different corner shops. Our journeys home from land to river have to be constantly remapped. Conversations, thoughts, dreams, nightmares; all now have a boating bent. The boat, and the water she traverses, are our obsession.

Braced, we eventually rise and set about making the cold boat warm. We had some foresight last night so there are ready-prepared layers beside the bed to step into: a t-shirt pre-nestled inside a jumper, a hooded sweater, ski socks and sheepskin boots. In the bathroom condensation laces across the window and beads up on the metal frame. The toilet seat is like ice. I shuffle into the kitchen in my too-big boots, and fill the kettle for tea and a wash. I tip porridge oats and milk into a saucepan and put it over a low heat. While both slowly reach the boil on the gas, the stove in the living room can be cleared of old ash and the fire laid and lit. It – closed, cast iron, with a glass window – is the heart of home and we forget this at our peril.

The boat squats long and low on the water. Flat-bottomed with a gently curving roof and traditional stern, she's a twenty-tonne hulk of metal painted black and midnight blue. Close inspection will reveal rusty war wounds and popped paint blisters; her crannies house snatches of cobweb and leaf. The boat's sides are protected by fenders fashioned from old car tyres, her bow and her stern cushioned with more traditional buttons of plaited black rope.

Unremarkable on the outside, it was the boat's innards that made us first fall for her. Inside she has country cottage charms. Dark wood floors, oak panelling, painted pine tongue and groove, built-in cabinets and plenty of brass. We bought her second-hand from a cabinet maker and his wife, who named her Pike as a wink to their gypsyish status. It's a moniker that will forever ingratiate us to freshwater fishermen. The couple designed and fitted the interior themselves. It shows. The more time you spend on board the more you realise it's the panelling or a shelf that's sitting at an off angle rather than the boat itself, but the cabin also has the handsome finish of a craftsman's hand and ingenious storage solutions only a boater would think of. Every step is hollow so it can double up as a chest; every nook realises its potential as a bookcase or cupboard. When the cabinet maker and his wife gave us our first tour, their love and pride felt strong. Age had overtaken them and they felt forced to give up the wandering life they had pursued since retirement. The five years they'd spent touring the UK canal network had infused Pike with an enthusiasm and practicality that we hoped would be infectious. This, we thought the minute we met her, was a boat with soul.

Two steep steps lead down into the living cabin from the front deck and it's important to mind your head as you climb in. The sides slope inwards and the oak ceiling has a gentle upward curve. As a whole the interior space has a shape similar to that of a tube train. The rooms adjoin in a long line, each a living space in its own right but also a connecting corridor to the next room along. The kitchen – or galley – is at the very front of the boat. It has fitted wooden cupboards down both sides, tiled worktops and a bar with high stools where we can eat. We have a power-hungry refrigerator that we only use in summer; in winter the cupboards are as cool as a fridge. There's a sink, an oven, a grill and a hob. It's the biggest kitchen I've had since moving to London at eighteen and I don't have to share it with anyone except the man that I love. The dirty dishes piled beside the sink and the shadowy smells of meals past are all our own.

The living room is next, on the other side of a frosted folding door. The walls are painted dark red and green, mixed with unpainted oak, and it is easily my favourite room. One corner is all bookcase and another all desk; there's a dresser and shelves on one side and a two-seat sofa on the other. The stove sits in this room, right in the middle of the boat, between the desk and a wooden coal box with daffodils carved into its lid. We have two ceiling-mounted drying racks by the chimney pipe, and a line stretched over the fire for wet towels and cloths. A large, fake Persian rug covers the floor, and a coffee table sits on top, stacked underneath with old newspapers and magazines. There are rectangular windows on both sides, curtained with thick floral fabric and lace. We dry out orange peel on the stovetop to mask some of the boat's earthier smells and are generally lazy about sweeping up. Everything, everywhere is gathering dust. It rolls in great soot balls down the hall and gathers in clumps around the rug.

A short oak-panelled and book-lined corridor links the sitting room to the bedroom, with the bathroom through a folding door to the side. We've painted the cabinets a creamy bright blue and decorated the white walls with pictures. There are all the things you would expect to find here: toilet, sink, shower, storage. The bedroom is larger and plainer, the walls painted off-white and the fitted wardrobes stripped pine. Our freestanding bed takes up most of the floor space but there's also room for more shelves and a chest.

Towards the back of the boat – the aft – there's a compact utility room with a porthole on each side and a large built-in coat cupboard, a chest of drawers, a washing machine, a small sink and space for bags and boots.

Finally there's the engine room, which is the equivalent of a chaotic garden shed. It's full of bicycle, wood and hose, and smells of diesel and grease. The doors swing right back and the top hatch slides across, opening out onto the small rear deck. The inside panels of our back doors are hand-painted with jumping silver-blue fish.

Pike's cabin is colourful and crowded but it isn't traditional and doesn't come close to the canal boat interiors that Barbara Jones depicts in *The Unsophisticated Arts*. In this book – a sketchbook really, and one that can be pored over for hours – Jones meticulously documents everyday, handmade art through illustrated essays and intricate pictures. It was first published in 1951, the same year Jones curated the 'Black Eyes and Lemonade' exhibition of British popular art at the Whitechapel Gallery, during the Festival of Britain. In a chapter called 'The Rose and the Castle', Jones celebrates and elevates the craft of canal boat decor, where strictly prescribed patterns extend inside as well as out. The now all-but-lost world she describes is splendid with painted decoration and dense ornament. Her busy drawings show cramped living cabins with every inch covered in hand-painted flowers, turrets and towers, and hung about with fussy lace-edged plates. The sketches also describe an exceptionally efficient use of space. In a family home that might have been just nine feet by seven – most of the boat being given over to cargo – everything would have its place and a dual purpose. The complexity of the decor belies the fact the paint job would have been executed swiftly and redone every three years because of intense wear and tear.

It's possible to experience a living cabin of similar dimensions first hand at the London Canal Museum, where a wooden narrowboat that worked between London and Birmingham in the 1930s is on display. The recreated cabin is truly tiny and just as efficiently organised as Barbara Jones describes, although not so lavishly decorated nor as layered with personal ornament. Here every piece of furniture doubles up as something else – fold-down cupboard doors become a dining table or a narrow bed – and there are lockers overhead and underneath. Sitting inside this boat, knees tucked up to chin and back hunched, it is mind-bending to imagine a family existing in such a confined space.

Jones' close study of canal boats' decoration leads her to theorise that 'only those that live such a separate and lonely life as that of canal boatmen will create elaborate layers of decoration round their daily lives'. The modern boating life is not nearly as isolated, which perhaps partly explains why boat interior design has so sobered up. Jones' documentary sketches capture a way of life soon to be wiped out by more modern logistics and tastes. Within twenty years the canals' commercial days had all but ended and those that lived aboard in such small but exuberant surroundings were forced to find other employment, and lodgings, on land.

We might not share the same visual style as Jones' boat people, nor indeed the same lifestyle, but we do negotiate a similarly shaped, if larger space. It's an interior you move through in a particular way, realigning your body to approach doors shoulder first, adopting your thinnest profile. Discounting the front and rear decks, Pike's living cabin is about 560 square feet – small, but in a capital city a respectable amount of space for two people. The fixtures and fittings stay solidly the same but the atmosphere inside the boat alters depending on where we're moored. The light and sounds filtering into the cabin space are distinct, each place we stop altering the colours of the fabrics and throwing different patterns up the walls and across the floor.

— ◆◆◆ —

It's Saturday. Afternoon already. The lie-in ended up spinning out until after twelve o'clock. S. takes charge of the fire and I spend some time looking out of the window while I wait for the water and the oats to heat up on the gas. The wind has temporarily dropped. Brown-grey and thick with debris, today the Lea sits flat and murky. Its headwaters are in the Chilterns just north of Luton and it cuts its course from Hertfordshire to the Thames at East India Dock with a lazy ease. This is no torrent, rushing headlong toward the sea. It's more of a slick, a swamp, a long thin pool. Wintering water birds bob through its solid seeming mass; barges and cruisers rock slowly in its barely-there ebb and flow. A half-submerged piece of wood floats by, an empty beer bottle in pursuit. Branches set free during recent high winds knit themselves with rogue plastic bags into slow-moving islands. Coots balance on top.

The UK is veined with over 2,000 miles of navigable canal and river like this. Now primarily used for recreation, the man-made network's industrial roots mean its waterways are a feature of towns and cities as much as the countryside. The Lea's fate has long been tangled up with our own and we have bent it to work to our will. For hundreds of years the tidal river system was an important source of food, water and power; the Domesday Book of 1086 records eight mills in the river's confusion of channels at Bow. The first lock was installed on the Lea at Waltham Abbey as early as 1576 and the true river was partially bypassed to form the Lee Navigation in 1769. The canalised stretch was then used as a route to and from the Thames by the 'stink industries', as Peter Ackroyd tellingly calls them in *Thames, Sacred River*. The naming is confusing but 'Lee' tends to be used for the canalised waterway and 'Lea' for the true river. Controlled by several locks and weirs but no longer hosting trade traffic, the River Lea and the Lee Navigation present different faces as they flow in and out of each other. The Lee is comparatively wide and straight, made practical for boats; the Lea meanders prettily.

This particular stretch of river beside Leyton Marsh – a stretch where the River Lea and the Lee Navigation are one – has long been sacred for continuously cruising boaters, those of us without permanent moorings who are licensed to journey on every two weeks. The bank here has room for around ten boats and is one of the only places to lower ropes within London that can really be called an urban wilderness; a hard-to-reach mooring where vessels are caressed by brambles yet Liverpool Street is minutes away by train. You can be in the heart of town one moment, doing London things, and out on the mist-shrouded marshes the next.

We will spend a fortnight here, paying close attention to lay of the land (meadow and marsh), the people (few) and the river's character (changeable), because we both want to and need to, and then we will move on. Our life is a continual departure. The boat is one of the only constants in it. We found her up north in June and were living on her down south by July. That hot summer long ago gave way to autumn, now winter. We have moored in many places over the intervening months; our most recent journey happened to end here. We like it. Other places feel less apart.

Once the fire is beyond babysitting point and we are fed, today we will do boat chores followed by a long bout of stove-side lounging. Outside the remnants of a heavy dew cling to the long grass, and there's the shadow of a slow-melting frost still stitched across the empty boat next door, our ghost ship neighbour that seems to have been left to ice up. The path running alongside the boat is narrow, uneven and, at the moment, muddy as hell. It's the kind of path you negotiate rather than stroll along; a path that snares you and snags your clothes. The slim length of canal verge wherever we moor can come to feel a little like our own ground, albeit temporarily. At Leyton Marsh the feeling is particularly strong because the main towpath runs along the opposite side of the river and, although this muddy path directly outside the boat is a public one, there is very little footfall here except our own. We are attached to the bank by way of ropes and long metal mooring pins at the bow and at the stern. It's a way of anchoring similar to that of guy ropes and tent pegs, but on a larger scale.

I have never lived in the countryside proper, somewhere remote and cut off, but I imagine ours as a rural kind of existence, especially in winter. It's a conceit I enjoy, one that is, of course, entirely misplaced in Zone 2. However, on a day like this one, you will likely find at least one of us out on deck or on the bank, steaming in thick woollens and walking boots as we split logs. It's harder work than it might look but there is satisfaction to be had in seasoned wood developing forking cracks under your will. Chase the cracks with the axe, make them widen and gape, until the trunk or branch splits down long ragged lines into stove-size pieces.

The goal this afternoon is to slice out enough slivers of wood to fill our hollow front steps. There is no shame in the fire-lighter but, even with that aid, plenty of good, dry kindling is key to starting a fire. It's a constant mission to keep supplies well stocked; we haunt the places where giant bins huddle on housing estates, hunting out old furniture and other flammable scraps. Skips are an endless source of offcuts. Our best find so far is an untreated, slatted pine bed, left discarded in bits on the pavement. And the most welcome Christmas present a dead tree from my dad's garden that was felled by a storm and then chainsawed into rough logs. It is this festive haul that we are axing apart today.

As well as being gifted logs and scavenging for our own, there are a handful of barges working up and down London's canals and rivers that deliver fuel and other boating paraphernalia direct. These fuel barges make life possible. We ordered coal and gas by text earlier this week and can now hear the fuel barge's lister engine put-putting upriver on the approach. It will pull up alongside us and plastic sacks of coal and a cylinder of gas will be hauled straight onto our roof. The barge will not only bring fuel but also news from the world beyond this riverbank. It cruises in the traditional twin formation of 72-foot narrowboat with 72-foot butty alongside. A butty is a narrowboat without an engine that doubles the available cargo space. Butty and boat move side by side, lashed together with ropes and powered by one engine. This particular pair are brightly painted with the green and red scales of the Welsh dragon. Both butty and boat have small cabins, where the couple who run the business live, but the vessels are mainly given over to goods: cylinders of gas, sacks of coal and a large tank of diesel. The fuel barge and its butty are a faint echo of the era when all the boats on London's canals were cargo-carrying ones.

The delivery is an excuse to spend some time on Pike's roof. It's our largest outside space but doesn't have the draw it does in summer. We use it mainly for storage at this time of year; there's a pallet where the coal sacks can be stacked and a tarp-covered top box for seasoning wood. It's also where we keep the gangplank, the lifebuoy, the boat poles and boat hooks, which we use for punting out of tight spots and fishing fallen things out of the water. I pace out our rectangular territory with its peaked nose and rounded back: 57 feet long and 10 feet across, about three feet wider than a narrowboat. I stand and keep watch for a while, my numb hands tucked up under my armpits. A dark grey barge passes heading north, its roof stacked high with branches brought down by the recent weather. The driver and I nod and smile.

Our own storm wood chopped, coal stacked and sun already sinking, we return to the cabin to enjoy the fire. When time is unimportant, tending the stove outstrips all other entertainment. A good fire, for us, often begins as a sandwich of newspaper, wood and coal. I call it coal for ease; it's actually a smokeless fuel suitable for cities. Still pitch black and phenomenally filthy, it comes in uniform, rounded square nuggets that burn with an odd odour. Paper and wood help light the nuggets and burn up fast with satisfying flames, but the ultimate goal is a pile of red glowing coals that fresh fuel can gradually be shovelled upon. Once the wood and paper have burned away and only coal remains, the smoke from our chimney should be barely discernible, just a faint distortion of hot air. We use logs too when we have them, and, depending on the tree, they usually burn much hotter than coal. It's not unknown for a log to reduce you to your underwear.

A back boiler helps to spread the warmth: water passes through pipes behind the stove where it heats up before being pumped into radiators in the bathroom and bedroom. We also have a device that uses a thermoelectric generator to convert heat from the stove into electricity. This powers a small motor, which in turn powers a fan that helps keep warm air inside the boat circulating. Both fan and boiler pump gently hum, our winter cicadas efficiently redistributing the stove's heat. This kind of technology holds much promise; we are now waiting for another stovetop device to be made for us that will convert heat energy into both a lamp and a charger for our laptops and phones.

Electricity is something we think about a lot. Our marine engine – like a tractor engine but for boats – tops up a bank of batteries that power the twelve-volt lights and plug sockets, and heats up water. In the summer we can rely on our rooftop solar panels to provide most of the power the batteries need but they can't keep up in winter, which is why channelling more thermoelectric energy from the stove would be brilliant. We obsessively monitor both the weather and our battery life at this time of year, rationing electricity use on the darkest days when we need it the most. Because daylight hours can be so very short, we have to run the engine for an hour most days to stop the batteries going flat. Outside you would barely notice it's on unless you got close but inside the whole boat vibrates with it, pots and pans jumping on the spot. There is an honesty in using the engine like this. On land you can easily forget that, with our current energy system, someone, somewhere has to burn something in order for the lights to come on or for the shower to run hot. On a boat without mains electricity, you have to burn the fuel yourself. It makes you much more conscious of what you're consuming.

Beyond physical dimensions, and creating one's own power and heat, daily life on board for us isn't so unlike life on land, although I think we are now more aware of how things work and the finiteness of things. When we plug something in we know exactly where the electricity has come from, and we know there's a possibility that the supply will stop. There's a feeling of precariousness that makes us appreciate small things like a light to read by or a hot shower more than we used to. I think the writer Tom Rolt's assertion that 'the boatman's life is stripped of all the complex comforts with which we have surrounded ourselves at the price of contentment' – a reflection of how his own experience living on a converted narrowboat in the 1930s compared to life on the land – just about holds true.[1] For Rolt, the spare life boating demands allows one to regain a lost sense of peace.

It is possible to surround yourself with complex comforts on a boat today, but it is easier than it would be on land to actively not. There is a paring back that takes place on the water, a simplification and an easing out. Our home space is not entirely domestic either; it is mechanical, it moves, it is subject to the weather, the water, the landscape. Richard Mabey was on to something when he said many of us – wherever we might live – nurse a 'dream of satisfying two strong and contrasting human drives, to be both settled native and adventurous pioneer'.[2] The boat allows us, demands us, to try to be both.

There's no doubt that this is a tough time of year to be living like this, that it's a season full of its own specific concerns. The fear of running out of fuel, of condensation and damp, of frozen pipes and flat batteries. The boat's climate is hard to control and our source of heat not instant or always reliable; sometimes the stove sulks and sighs and fills the cabin with smoke. And everything breaks in winter. Last week the folding bathroom door fell off the wall in a weary heap, just like that. There are, however, some advantages to the cold. For a would-be hermit like me, it's welcome to have the excuse to stay in, fire tending, self-importantly fending off the chill while rain blears the windows and makes the outside invisible. The cabin is lovely in candle- and firelight, the cosiest place you could possibly be. Flame light is forgiving, it hides all the cracks.

Night comes early at this time of year and an evening passes in much the same way anyone else's might: a meal, the radio, a film, the washing up, a book. The sky has cleared tonight and a full moon trails across the water, beaming uninterrupted through our front doors. I wonder if, when I was a house dweller, I ever felt quite so close to the stars.

On the stovetop the samovar quietly hisses, the gathering heat bubbles making the copper sing. I move it onto a trivet to stop the water boiling and fetch a jug from the bathroom so the hot liquid can be decanted out. I need a wash. The living room is warm, the bathroom cool in comparison. The water creates clouds as it fills the sink, fogging the mirror opaque. I clean the day from my face and hands, wiping away the coal and the wood dust, carefully flushing out a new wound on my left forefinger. I slipped earlier with the axe, my one false move met with a flash of red pain and a small crescent-shaped gash. Living on a canal boat marks you out in this way. Cuts and splinters, a thumb knuckle seared white, fingernails ingrained with grime, smoke-laced hair: these are all the necessary side effects of keeping a vessel warm. Clean, I return to the stove-side to undress before scurrying into the back cabin, to boyfriend and bed. Beneath two duvets and a huge blanket, S. and I keep each other warm. The fire burns out as we sleep.

3. fen

London is a city of contrasts. Here in the borough of Waltham Forest, one of Britain's most polluted rivers runs alongside one of the capital's last remaining wetlands, part of which is designated a Site of Special Scientific Interest. Perhaps this peculiarity is part of the Lower Lea's charm: that it is an unexpected pleasure and a bit of a mess at the same time. The river is loved and well used by all sorts of people – rowers, runners, walkers, cyclists, motor boaters like me – even when wintry conditions are harsh, but it's also shamefully abused. Every day great islands of rubbish float past. Some of it is likely to be accidental blow-off, lightweight stuff that has been caught by the wind, but things like insulation panels seem purposefully dumped. The snarled-up weir downriver from here, below Lea Bridge, illustrates just how much junk ends up in the water. The flotsam that accumulates is only part of the picture; it doesn't show the pollution from roads and houses with misconnected pipes that lurks in the water as well.

The River Lea is especially vulnerable in wild weather as storm run-off from roads flows straight into it from across east London. In July 2013, when two weeks of hot, dry weather were followed by torrential rain, a cocktail of oil, copper, lead, zinc, grit and tar flooded into the river because there was no buffer to filter the flow. Dissolved oxygen levels, which were already low because of the heat, dropped to zero in places. Thousands of fish died.[3]

Despite horrors like this, the Lea – which, with its streams, forms London's second largest river system – still manages moments of beauty. It can support many species of bird and fish; there are rumours that bitterns, kingfishers, even water voles frequent its banks. At the moment, on cold mornings and nights, the water is often cloaked with great puffs of organza-soft mist.

Walthamstow and Leyton Marshes lie low in the river's alluvial flood plain on a bed of silt, gravel and London clay. They don't have the curves and contours the name Lee Valley suggests. They're flat, soggy expanses, crisscrossed by railway lines and ringed with industry. A line of poplar trees marks the border between the two. The marshes have a wildlife-rich bleakness about them at this time of year. Over 400 species of plant have been recorded here, with 250 considered regulars. There's meadow, reed bed and wooded thicket as well as marshland, which together attract snipe, water rail, stonechat and meadow pipit in winter.[4]

Both marshes have fraught pasts and even today their future doesn't feel completely secure. There seems always to be someone willing to sacrifice our green spaces for profit. Before Site of Special Scientific Interest designation in the mid-1980s, gravel extraction loomed large at Walthamstow Marsh. It was, incredibly, the Lee Valley Regional Park Authority that applied to the Greater London Council for permission to dig down 36 feet, mine the marsh for its gravel and then replace it with a marina. Threats do, thankfully, spur bursts of action and, now and then, the activists are victorious.

Michael Knowles – one of many involved in saving Walthamstow Marsh – recently produced a pamphlet that tells the story of the campaign and how it was won through creativity, high spirits and hard work. In it, he describes the site as it is today as 'a monument to what a determined group of people, even when confronted by the powers of the land, can achieve'. He also cautions that we 'remain constantly aware of this precious and cherished feature' and 'be always on guard against the false blandishments of transient profit or ephemeral pleasure' that could threaten it again.

The pamphlet is a defiant quest for the local people

who saved the marsh to be properly acknowledged but also a personal exercise in remembering, a way of solidifying the past within the pages of a self-published book. Knowles spent a lot of time on the marshes and beside the river in the 1970s, and shares some of his strongest recollections, including one that describes the Lea's recent industrial past:

There were few sights I can recall so magnificent, so locked into my mind's eye, as that of the great barges pushing their way through the water, sailing up from the Thames through the Isle of Dogs, loaded with huge logs, which had been unloaded in the London docks and transferred onto the barges, making their way to the timber yards, the waves they created rising up against the prow and splashing over the decks. It was splendid honest physical work; and the sight of it all on a frosty winter morning, the sun gleaming and dancing in the waves and the surging resisting waters, is simply unforgettable.[5]

Beyond the survival of Walthamstow Marsh itself, one of the most valuable products of the Save the Marshes campaign was a detailed wildlife survey, first produced in 1979 and updated at the end of 1980. It's an important record of the species the marshes supported 35 years ago, but it also expresses something deeper that locals drew from their 'fen in the city'. The document reads as a sparkling ode to 'a piece of countryside of extraordinary antiquity' as well as an ecological survey. The authors describe a place of wonder, somehow just about unscathed by a hundred years of industrialisation; somewhere 'created by nature over the course of many centuries', where 'ancient water meadow has survived largely intact as if by a miracle'.[6]

Their awe lives on. It still seems phenomenal that this east London marshland has largely escaped development, and that it survives is supremely important. As Iain Sinclair says in *London Orbital*, in a chapter entitled 'Soothing the seething', 'without the Lea Valley east London would be unendurable'. It is one of the city's natural healing forces, one that keeps all of us who know it sane. It certainly soothes me.

But we shouldn't be calmed into complacency, and we must remember to heed Knowles' warning about transient profits and ephemeral pleasures. The marshes' existence cannot be taken for granted. Leyton Marsh – or Porter's Field Meadow as it is sometimes known – is still recovering from a recent land grab. Despite being designated Metropolitan Open Land, the landowners – again, the

Lee Valley Regional Park Authority – allowed a basketball training facility to be built on it to cater for the 2012 Olympics. Local people were outraged and campaigned against it, but this time to no avail.[7] The always temporary but always intrusive construction has since been removed and users are now on guard against further incursions, mobilised as the Save Lea Marshes group. Further south, East Marsh was concreted over to make way for an Olympic coach park, again temporary but again out of place.[8]

— ◆◆◆ —

A grey heron sweeps in. It lands on a branch newly overhanging the water – a storm casualty – and at once adopts a stance that is taut, stretched out and perfectly still, its sharp eyes fixed on the water. Neck plume ruffling in the building breeze. Its long yellow-orange-pink bill poised patient for the fast strike when, if, a fish comes. The author Iain Sinclair watches herons hunting along the Lea too. For him, the slender birds are 'neo-Romantic doodles', with 'scissor-beaks and Anglepoise knees'.[9]

I sometimes see what I think is the shadow of a fish passing beneath the boat, but it's hard to get a grasp of what's going on underwater. I rely on fishermen's reports: barbel, bream, chub, common carp, dace, eel, flounder, gudgeon, perch, pike, roach, ruffe and sea trout are all listed as catches on the Lea, although I'm unsure exactly which part of the river. The heron's return visits suggests there is something worth waiting for in this spot. The bird is aloof, focused, independent, a serious predator, always alone.

I first got to know London's large grey heron community in town, at Regent's Park, where the birds are ubiquitous and behave just like the pigeons and the ducks. I lived and studied close by and would regularly do a circuit through the rose garden and around the lake. There was a nun who used to visit the herons daily, bringing sprats fresh from the fishmongers. The herons seemed to recognise her tiny form from a distance, her specific shuffle step and the swing of the blue plastic bag she carried, full of stinking fish. Her affection for the birds was even-handed but ran deep; she said she felt guilt on the days when her duties meant she couldn't come, she shared the food as equitably as she could, and she addressed the huge birds as they flocked around her as though they were her kith and kin. There's been a heronry at Regent's Park since 1968, which has grown in line with the bird's national increase.[10] This solitary heron fishing close to the boat on the River Lea seems a world apart.

There's only so long you can spend on deck heron-watching before you attract the attention of the patrolling, always hopeful, local waterfowl. Two Canada geese swim over, flagging a food source to a pair of swans and a coot. I'd never looked deep into goose eyes before they became neighbours, nor realised I could enjoy their company quite so much. Like the nun with her herons, I anthropomorphise them horribly and patronise them like pets, chastising their greed one moment, indulging it the next. While the coots remain territorial, even they seem more relaxed at the moment, free from the pressure to mate, guard eggs or care for young. Swans often float past abandoned to sleep, their long necks curled up under the wing. They herd together in large numbers upriver, no longer quite so graceful-looking when in a pack.

Dipping back down into the cabin I realise that it's going to be hard to leave this mooring spot beside Leyton Marsh, with its wild marshlands so nearby, its birds and its sense of privacy that isn't easy to find anywhere else. An attachment develops in a matter of days. It's interesting just how quickly we can settle into a landscape and call it home. We moored here once before, in summer. The marshes have an entirely different demeanour in the heat. In July Walthamstow is a tall tapestry of green and yellow, purple and rust. Bush vetch tussles with everlasting pea and wild honeysuckle. Reedmace thrusts. The insects are giddy and drunk. It's a far starker place in winter but still beautiful.

This is one of the only places in London where we can have the curtains and blinds open on both sides of the boat.

It's refreshing to look out without the danger of someone else looking in. (Who can resist peering into a houseboat when they get the chance?) The riverbank is high, obscuring the marshes beyond, so the views aren't panoramic. What we see is buddleia, brambles and elm, close up, with the occasional rainbow flash of low sun on starling. The branches reach right up to the windows and squeal across the glass every time Pike shifts back and forth between her ropes. The starlings' feathers have an iridescent sheen like oil on dark water and their bellies are speckled with fading white dots, their autumn markings slowly wearing off. They are boisterous neighbours. The birds were once much more common in London; great flocks would descend on the city centre at dusk. It's hard to imagine a murmuration in Leicester Square, but such things did happen. There's a story that one evening in 1949 the birds had the audacity to land on the face of Big Ben, causing the clock to stop.[11] The starling population has dropped by 70 per cent since then, due to a lack of food and nesting sites, and the bird is now a red listed species.[12] It's becoming a rare thing to live with them so close at hand.

We have been moored on Leyton Marsh's edge for a while now and S. and I discuss moving on. When will we do it? Where will we go? We will leave soon but not right now, we decide. We're both working tonight – S. at a pub in town, me reviewing a play – and so, we think, this afternoon let's just get out of our steel box. Let's console ourselves with a walk across wide empty space in strong wind. Let's listen to gusts so loud it's impossible to think of anything else, especially where next. There will be reeds and sedges up to our armpits, and a gape of grey sky that is vast. The land will be spongy and sodden, and red duckweed will have matted over the ditches and turned the water into wine.

We decide to walk to Walthamstow town. First over the cattle grid and along the river, following the gravel track. Then onto the boardwalk straight into the marsh's heart. Next we follow the muddy pathways and spray-painted foot tunnels to Springfield Marina, then turn right down Coppermill Lane, past the chain-linked-in reservoirs with their fantastical island colonies of cormorants and herons. The birds' poo has singed and stunted the trees into prehistoric black stumps. It's a cold, damp trudge but, after a few days confined to the boat by the weather and our own lassitude, open space and exercise are a welcome relief. When we are spent, we take the train back to Clapton, dirty water sprayed disgracefully up our legs and our backs.

Later I leave the boat again to go to the theatre, this time dressed up and made up, wrapped inside a long black coat.

I fix plastic bags over my new suede ankle boots with elastic bands to get me clean to the bus. The journey into town allows me time to transition from marsh person into something else, someone more in tune with the inner city. Sitting in the playhouse, I get a whiff of myself. Unwashed hair and woodsmoke. Distracted, I glance down and in the half-light see a fine mist of mud sprayed across the coat folded neatly in my lap.

On my way out of town again much later that night, when I transition back to marsh person once more, the bus drops me at an ice rink and the walk home is a necessarily isolated one. Midnight strolls have undeniable appeal but, solo, this one is tainted with concerns about getting mugged and nobody being around to hear my screams. I wear my collection of keys like a knuckleduster and entertain violent thoughts. The most direct route is through the ice rink's deserted car park and out into empty marshland. Tonight the moon is shaded by cloud that's dyed orange-pink by distant city and suburban lights. It's gloomy and damp, with foliage that lurches and creaks in the wind. I walk fast down the gravel track with the river on my left, Leyton Marsh spreading out on my right and my heart in my mouth.

Despite the nerves, I manage to revel in the fresh air after the steamed-up and clammy night bus, to enjoy the way the foggy chill slips between layers and tickles at the skin. London's thieves surely wouldn't be brave enough to lie in wait out here tonight, it's too cold and dank and dark. I briefly fall in step with a fox before she swaps gravel for grass. I flick on my torch. The small circle of light dances across dense hedgerow, seeking out the right gap. Once found, the path through the undergrowth and down to the river edge is treacherous. I slow my pace and, one tentative step at a time, make it to the bow, the plastic bags covering my boots now slick with fresh mud. Our wet ropes have slackened and the gap between bank and boat is bigger than usual. I grip the roof with my hands and pull myself off the slippery path onto the front deck. The river gently buffets Pike, the quick laps a welcome back pulse. I pull off the muddy bags, stoop down through the doors and into the cabin, adrenalin pumping like I've conquered the night.

4. river

The Thames, of course, is London's most iconic
attribute. It has always been a fundamental part
of the city's geography and psyche. The River, as it is
simply known, continues to run wide and fast through
Londoners' hearts. But we don't go there, although we
could. It's not our chosen territory. As mighty as it is, it
doesn't exist in isolation; there are tributaries, natural and
man-made. We stick to these backwaters, the ditches that
score the landscape to the north. The Thames is the father
they all feed into but each has a life of its own. The narrow seams of the Grand Union, Regent's Canal and River
Lea once heaved with trade traffic and were banked by
factories and wharves. Today they heave with houseboats
and are overlooked by blocks of flats. They are domestic,
and a little bit wild.

We will move Pike today, to somewhere along the Lee
Navigation, but a friend has called to tell us he will visit
this morning and that he is bringing breakfast. So we wait.
Jack lives on a boat up at the marina and we're not far off.

He will cycle, I expect, and be here in ten minutes, maybe less. It has been months since we last met and he hasn't even seen our boat yet. He knows nothing of our current life. How do I manage to neglect my friends in this way? Or allow them to neglect me? Ten minutes pass. The kettle boils and begins to cool off. We resort to cereal and wonder where he's got to but resist the urge to check. Things more important than us can crop up.

A boat approaches from the north, heading slowly downriver. It's a thrill when we realise that it's him, that he's decided to travel to us by water not track. Jack's home is much lovelier-looking than ours: a small Dutch working boat, retired, with a wheelhouse on top that doubles up as a conservatory. She's the perky shape of a tugboat you might draw, boxy on top and curvy below. Jack pulls alongside and flings over some ropes. We tie his vessel onto ours, before heading inside to turn the parcel of earthy portobellos and sourdough he presents into buttery fried mushrooms on toast. We manage to fill an hour with nothing but boat and river talk, and then we are untying his ropes and pushing off and hoping the wind won't make the return journey too challenging. As Jack and his boat slowly disappear north, we resume our journey south.

I love pitching off somewhere new, into the unknown,

but move days still give me the fidgets. We know the direction we are headed but we never know quite where we'll end up. Boat trips, whatever their compass, often bring out what Kathleen Winter calls in *Boundless* that 'tension between freedom and belonging'. It's a curious feeling, exciting and uncertain. If we can't find anywhere to moor, we might just journey on and on until we slip off the edge.

I moved house five times as a child and after leaving home at eighteen there were seven more moves to rooms around London. All that sorting, packing and throwing away. The hundreds of cardboard boxes and the reels of sticky brown tape. The up and down and back and forth. The starting all over again. Twelve moves in 30 years, every one of them emotional. On Pike we move about twenty times a year. Obviously Pike is our home and she comes with us wherever we go, it's only the location that changes. But still, it's a ruptured way of living. We have chosen a life that means we can live in several places over the course of a month, a year – a life full of the liberating possibilities of having more than one postcode – but we have also chosen a life where we are constantly being shooed on. A move is generally initiated because we've stayed in a place for the maximum length of time allowed or because we've run out of water, or both. In this way our journeys are largely functional, although that doesn't mean they aren't also fun.

We step off the boat and onto the towpath to do the ropes – S. takes care of the back, I do the front. They're still wet from the rain. First we untie our careful knots, unloop the ropes and tug out the mooring pins. I stay on the muddy path holding the front rope, S. coils up the back rope and positions himself on the stern, tiller in hand, ready to steer us out into the water. At his signal I throw the front rope on board and then push Pike's nose out into the channel, one foot on the gunwale and one on the bank, two hands on Pike. We need to ensure we will clear the neighbouring boats. Once I reach maximum stretch point, I swing myself onto the front deck, coil up the front rope ready for later and then join S. at the back as he powers us out into the river. We have developed a neat little launch routine that makes me feel like we know what we're doing, when it works. Today everything goes smoothly and now we are off.

We travel with no predetermined end point in mind and with only a few criteria as to where to stop: somewhere where boats are already moored, where there's a gap big enough for Pike to fit and, ideally, where we think we'll get a decent amount of sun on our solar panels. Pike moves through the water slowly and efficiently, without creating much of a wash. It's a sliding sort of a movement. Not elegant but not inelegant either. Certainly not dramatic. Just simple, I suppose. We get overtaken by cyclists but maintain a pace a little bit faster than walking. There is opportunity to fully take in the surroundings, to view them from the middle of the river rather than the edge. A woman watches us approaching from high up on a footbridge, her ears muffled beneath oversized headphones, her body bundled in fake fur and striped wool. We exchange a wave. She seems miles off. Out here we have our own rhythm and occupy our own time and space, distant from everyone else.

We follow the river as it bends into a tight 'S' before splitting in two just after passing under Lea Bridge Road. It's a clear morning and low winter sun beats the water into blinding liquid gold, cleansing the landscape of its ugly A-route. My hands turn blue and my nose glows red. S. draws me in, one arm on the tiller, one hooped round my waist. We continue along the canalised Lee Navigation while its twin, the River Lea proper, now flows free of boats to our left. The two waterways fork away from each other but, once separate, they run parallel south. They cut along either side of a nature reserve known as the Middlesex Filter Beds, a name that echoes its original Victorian use in a time of cholera.

A high brick wall forms a barrier between the woodland and reed bed of the reserve and the Navigation's towpath. As we continue downriver, the wall ends, wrought iron railings begin and the land opens out into Hackney Marsh, which is basically a large playing field but one with wooded skirts and water flowing along each of its long edges. The marsh has the feel of an island, one that's flat and wide enough to fly a kite, do a cartwheel or run like the wind, with no fear of crossing anyone's path. Crows are dotted everywhere, big black full stops that suddenly start and rise as one at some hidden signal. White football and rugby goalposts sprout irregularly and often from the close-cropped grass; pagan, skeletal, standing stones. On the other side of the Navigation is a pungent dustbin lorry park and Lower Clapton's warren of estates and steep sloping terraces.

When a suitable space to moor comes into view, we enact the launch process in reverse. I head to the bow of the boat. S. swings the back out so the nose can approach the bank. I jump to shore with a rope. Safely on land, I hold the front rope loosely so the nose can swing back out and allow S. to guide the stern in. Once the back end is close enough to the bank, S. leaps off with the other rope and then together we pull her tight in to the towpath by hand. We hammer mooring pins into the soft canal verge at the front and rear, then loop our ropes through them and back onto the boat. We tie our best knots, making sure the ropes are left loose and long enough to cope with any changes in the water level. We reposition our fenders to suit the new bank and to make a buffer on our outer side should someone pull alongside us.

The last job before we can relax is to check the weed hatch and untangle anything that has become caught in the propeller. It's important to do this after a trip as we drive through an awful lot of flotsam and some of it is bound to get trapped. The weed hatch is very tightly secured and I can only undo it with a hammer. Once it's open, it's possible to reach down through the boat, into the river and access the propeller. We have unwound a depressing amount of plastic from it as we've travelled through London. Once the prop is clear, and the weed hatch hammered back into place, we're done. I take in our new location. Beer cans are speared in a row on the railing spikes, an ill-judged boast; across the water a community garden with big raised beds runs along the water's edge.

The area around the Lee Navigation in this spot is known locally as 'the Filter Beds', named after the nature reserve. The ecologist David Goode describes in *Wild in London* how he was first tipped off about its existence in August 1982. Rumour had it that the derelict waterworks, which had closed in 1969 after more than a hundred years' service, were running wild. Intrigued enough to visit, he admits he 'was not prepared for the changes which could occur in such a place once it is totally abandoned'. There was no obvious way in and his view was obstructed by the tall brick wall. Finding a concrete block to stand on so he could peer over the top, Goode's eyes met 'a scene of total tranquility', of ponds, reed beds and willow. I imagine him now, on tiptoe, straining to drink in all that was occurring over the high walls. He sees mallards, coots, moorhens, a heron, a large brown dragonfly, several reed warblers, a party of goldfinches, a kingfisher and a kestrel overhead.

He visited again and again, soon discovering a hole in the fence used by birdwatchers and locals 'who enjoy the solitude of the place'. Now able to wander through the site and catalogue its contents in more detail, he concluded that within 'little more than ten years, some 30 different marshland plants have colonised the filter beds, creating a colourful mixture of wetland habitats from scratch'. Later, during the winter of 1982–3, he would see snipe, lapwing, mallard, teal, pochard, tufted duck, gadwall, shoveler and ringed plover.

For a while the abandoned waterworks belonged to the birds and the lucky few who knew, but the site became more open after part of the towpath wall collapsed. By the time Goode wrote his book four years later, it was 'less of a sanctuary for birds, more of an unofficial wetland wilderness for many local people'. Such a place was clearly something Londoners wanted. Today it is very much official, complete with signboards, way markers and a proper gate. It's a popular part of people's daily dog walks and sometimes a place to illicitly gather after dark. On a damp day in winter, when fair-weather walkers keep away, it's still possible to have its cool woody reaches all to yourself.

On the other side of the nature reserve, the true River Lea presents a more picturesque face than the Navigation. It has shallow edges and gently shelving banks. It meanders through rocky outcrops, gravelly patches and odd explosions of giant hogweed. I like to stand on the footbridge at the north-eastern corner of Hackney Marsh and watch the water animate its long manes of underwater weed. The way the plants snake and writhe is hypnotic. Winding pathways connect river, woodland and field with the nature reserves and further marshland to the north. It's a large, varied, wondrous landscape that is never anything other than urban. There are roads and light industry, a sewage pipe, a metal security fence and a concrete underpass. This is the grubby edge of a huge city after all.

We moor in this blurry marginal place – an ecotone, and in ways not just biological. Dry land meets water, yes, and city meets nature too. But also, for us, public meets private. After the relative isolation of Leyton Marsh, Pike is now much more conspicuous, moored as she is against a busy towpath. Standing at the kitchen sink, we might witness ten, twenty, 30 pairs of feet walk, run or cycle past, or lock eyes with a dog. The Venetian blinds on the towpath side are twisted almost shut but it's still possible to see shadows beyond and the thin blurred strip of someone, something, moving past. On the water side the blinds are open and we witness a steady stream of waterfowl, rowers, other barges and boats.

His thoughts are in north-west London when he writes, and not in this decade, but Richard Mabey's short book *A Good Parcel of English Soil* somehow captures the atmosphere of this contemporary towpath territory well. In it, Mabey recalls his suburban childhood and an environment where 'the border between the domestic world and the wild was porous and mobile'; he later describes the 'ecologically potent badlands' surrounding the urban canal close to his workplace. Both descriptions speak to me of what's going on outside the boat here. They capture the landscape's mutability: the way industry, humanity and wildness intermingle. Pike sits in a public park, on a public waterway, alongside a public footpath. Densely packed housing on one side, wide-open space on the other.

In this volatile landscape – in these porous, potent bad-lands – inside the boat, we continue to create our first home as before. We pore over the details of our new-found domesticity, deliberating about how best to shape our private space. The humours and shades of the water and the marshes are informing our choices, from the kinds of pictures we pick for the walls and the books we decide to read, to the blue-grey striped bed linen and the slate-coloured towels. Even the inherited Hornsea teacups seem made to be drunk from in this place; cups the colour of moss and mud, and wet all over with glaze.

5. unreal city

Light fails well before the working day ends. The ride home from my studio to the riverside takes me down through residential Lower Clapton and straight across Millfields Park, where bike lights beam into a white-out of wet fog. The temperature drops as you descend into the gully, and the air becomes fumey and damp. Millfields made me nervous at first but now I love the sensation of leaving the real world behind at this point; it has come to feel safer than the roads at night. Pedal fast through its swirling vapours, turn right where the park ends and the towpath begins, go over the neat little footbridge and into the smoke-smelling dark, and there you'll find a rare unlit part of London and a group of slim, path-hugging boats, their orange-lit 'O's punching holes into the deepening gloom.

On Pike we work hard to keep the living cabin warm and dry. Condensation is becoming a problem so we install moisture traps in every room. The kitchen is worst; the wooden spoons keep growing fuzzy white beards and the cupboards and their contents are coated with cold sweat. The galley is the only part of the boat, aside from the engine room, that the fire doesn't really heat; the room warms up when we cook but meal preparations always begin with the chef in a scarf and a hat. We'll take any excuse to have the oven on for an hour and so there are far more roasts and bakes in our diet than before. Over dinner this evening we discuss the fact we haven't filled up with water for several weeks, and where we might move to next. The closest tap is at Hackney Wick. We use a dipstick to measure the depth of water in the tank and predict we can probably last another week but decide to move closer to the tap tomorrow nevertheless.

From the Filter Beds we will follow the Lee Navigation as it cuts down through Homerton, a stretch of river that feels fairly grim at first glance but that you come to appreciate. The most southerly part of Hackney Marsh crouches on one side of Homerton Road Bridge – the wind breathing erratic life into its great pelt of bushes and trees – and Wick Wood spreads out on the other. I have watched the passing of an unusual and probably ancient wooden narrowboat moored along here with morbid interest over the last few weeks. Rotten right through, her bow eventually split, she filled with water and sank. The Navigation is shallow, so her fractured carcass is still visible even though her hull is on the riverbed. Painted in classic canal boat colours, her peeling greens and reds are fast fading but hint at a glorious past. It's been a dark, fascinating disintegration, a slow public falling apart that induces a great deal of anxiety. I don't consciously consider the possibility of Pike sinking all that much but every time I see this sad totem it brings on the night sweats.

We move the boat to a position below the wreck and between two road bridges the next day, opposite a terrace of blank houses and beside Wick Wood. We've made home here before. There's a bench with magnetic powers that many passers-by cannot resist; the space beneath it rolls with cans and ash. Boats are an essential part of this scene, strung all along one side. People often come to this area when they need to fix something, mooring in the shelter of the A12 as it flies over the river. At night there are bodiless voices under the bridges, and the whine of puny motorbikes in the woods.

Arriving in a new part of town every two weeks means getting to know what utilities are available locally. I am building a map of these things in my head, a network of amenities that can be relied on, like food shops and laundrettes. We have a washing machine on Pike, but we rarely have the water or electricity needed to power it, so we have to clean our clothes and bedding elsewhere.

Sitting on an uncomfortable bench in the bright light of a laundry helps focus thoughts. The rotations of washing in a machine make you lose them again. In a house or a flat you are unlikely to watch your washing as it spins, but in a laundrette it's hard not to. I've discovered I can easily spend an hour studying the rise and fall of wet clothes. That sweater looks peculiar, saturated and manipulated, a soaked puppet that's lost its hands and its head.

The coin-op laundrette closest to our new spot in Homerton is, I think, based on my admittedly limited research, the cheapest in London. Today it is empty apart from the proprietress with her heavy kohl eyes that won't meet mine, and a thin, creased man who sits in the corner chuckling and muttering. She makes mugs of tea for them both and then stands in the doorway to smoke, only allowing herself half a cigarette before carefully squeezing it out and slotting it back in the packet for later. Rather than retreating into the book I've brought along, I instead read the heavily scored price lists tacked on the walls and multifarious messages 'from the Management', before falling into a reverie about laundries I've visited in the recent past.

There's the laundrette on Mare Street, hectic with pot plants and posters, which had an attentive attendant who paced the length of the laundry over and over, and stared for long, longing minutes out of the window. He was kind, helped me fold up my bed sheets. And there's the laundry in Clapton, which I last used on New Year's Eve afternoon. What a place to find oneself on such a day, although necessary if I was to achieve my resolution of starting 2014 beneath freshly laundered sheets. I thought it would be quiet but it was packed, most people coming in with washed but wet clothes, creating a long queue for the industrial dryers. One woman did no washing or drying at all, just wrote solidly in a notebook. A character in search of characters, or a warm place to sit.

A family arrived, parents with their grown-up children. There was the crick and lisp of a lager opening and it snowballed from there. The atmosphere grew raucous and a little tense. This laundrette was unusually unattended, there was nobody around to provide change for a fiver or curb anyone's enthusiasm. I sat and waited and watched sheets encircle each other, bubble, expand and contract, before tackling the more active frustrations of the tumble dryer, which demanded an endless flow of 20ps to get the bedclothes beyond warm and wet. Laundrettes – a feature of most cruising boaters' lives – are a source of pleasure and pain. There's nothing quite like clean sheets.

S. suggests a walk in the woods, good compensation for hours lost to laundry. Wick Wood is a young woodland squeezed into the triangle created by Homerton Road, the A12 and the Lee Navigation. We can step off the boat and into it in a few paces, and we set out along a path that follows its diagonal edges. It's a kind of cloud forest at the moment, in the way that it is dripping wet and blanketed with a haze of fine drizzle. Once known as Wick Field, it was planted into a community woodland in the late 1990s. There's a mix of black poplar, oak, apple, ash, willow, plane, cherry, birch and hazel. The alders are strung with female catkins and consequently busy with siskins, yellow-green finches that love to eat the seeds inside the tiny cone-like fruits. Their song is a 'high-energy liquid cacophony'.[13] A local birdwatcher whom we find in the undergrowth tells us all about them, talking at length about his patch and encouraging us in our novice ornithology. Branching off the outer path, where the traffic noise is difficult to ignore, it's possible to lose yourself more completely. Towards the heart of the wood is an opening where the trees have been coppiced into toadstool-ish stumps. There are shelters woven from willow and heaps of curled shavings, remnants of a spoon whittling class. Urban bushcraft sessions are still in vogue. We're always considering future fires and so stuff our pockets with a few choice curls as we pass.

This woodland walk is muddy, and mud is an anomaly in London, even across the road from this wonderland of leaf mulch and vegetal filth. We tramp from the woods over the bridge and straight into the local mini-market, where our dirty boots and mist-matted hair are met with silent disgust. The shop sits at the back and bottom of a huge new, sun-blocking complex of flats called Matchmaker's Wharf, almost completely hidden from sight and with no signs to direct you its way. We are led here, like some sort of Hansel and Gretel, by a trail of blue plastic bags. The shop is unusual in that it is independent and family-run. Numerous new developments in London sit above big-name supermarkets or café chains, but not here. This store has its own butcher and sells fresh Turkish bread and olives, cheap wine and every salty snack under the sun. It's an excellent addition to my mind map of useful corner shops. We buy food for dinner and tramp back to the boat just as the rain sets in. The river is elastic with it, each heavy drop pushing and pulling at the surface, rousing it into bouncing peaks and troughs. The boat is drubbed to even darker shades of black and blue.

I arrange to walk in Wick Wood again with Katelyn, a dyer and designer who knows it well. We roamed about together a few summers ago, when the grass was hip-height and the 2012 Olympics still a whole year off. It was a gorgeous Saturday then, the first day of sun after a few days of rain, and the wood was bright green and lush, full of tree tunnels and vigorous nettle clumps, their leaves young and fresh. Katelyn wore lace-up brown ankle boots and a billowing white cotton dress, hand-embroidered with sprays of blue flowers. In her bike trailer were rubber gloves, secateurs, cooking pots and a portable gas stove. She harvested bundles of nettles, stuffing them into a huge cooking pot to be boiled in water to make a green-yellow dye. She also dug up a dock root, explaining that while it may need to be cooked for several hours to release the colours, the resulting rusty pinks, shimmering golds and autumnal oranges would be worth it. In a world dominated by yellows, natural dyers come to prize the reds.

I quickly realised that Katelyn's way of looking at a landscape was different from my own. Where I saw gradients of brown and green, she saw the potential for ombre, chestnut and gold, for mustard, terracotta and mink. She showed me that there's more to this wood than the surface presents. Katelyn didn't walk so much as rummage; she didn't follow the path but zig-zagged out her own confusing route. She explained that foraging for dye plants is, for her, all about paying attention and monitoring a local patch. Katelyn approaches her work as though it were its own ecosystem, delighting in the fact something as common as nettle can be a food, a fibre and a dye.

We find an excuse to meet and so explore Wick Wood

together again, this time as winter reluctantly gives itself over to spring. A walk in the woods with Katelyn involves rootling about in the undergrowth, whatever the weather. It's not a good time of year for leafy plants, so instead she teaches me about the colours that can be squeezed out of trees. The bark from young, fallen cherry branches can produce dyes that range from pinks and oranges to greens and golds. Elder's bark creates a delicate metallic pink. The inner bark of birch produces a pinky brown, while the outer bark gives a lighter, subtler shade. Katelyn explains that natural dyes change in different lights. They shimmer with a richness and depth that synthetic colours often lack.

As we wander, I find I still envy Katelyn her close connection to this place, the fact her understanding of it runs so detailed and deep, but I think I have achieved some of her ability to find meaning in this river valley in the intervening years since we last met. She has her dyeing, I have my boat. Pike forces me into a closer kind of contact with the landscape every day and so I, slowly, forge out a relationship with it that feels like it too has colour and depth.

— ◆◆◆ —

South of the A12, the Lee Navigation continues through to Hackney Wick and Old Ford Lock. The River Lea proper, which we lost somewhere behind Hackney Marsh, has split into a series of separate waterways now, known collectively as the Bow Back Rivers. The once hidden, fly-tipped semi-tidal channels have become the much-hyped centrepiece of the Queen Elizabeth Olympic Park.[14] Here is another volatile place. This area is contentious and has been since 2007, when London won its Olympic bid and the big blue fence went up. The Back Rivers were shut off to boats and remain closed to this day, their promised reopening postponed and their character irretrievably changed.

Since summer 2012 few will publicly speak ill of the Games. All those gold medals, the commitment to the brand, the manicured landscape with its carpets of wildflowers as far as the eye could see – who could fail to be impressed? But the Olympic project was not universally welcomed, and its ongoing dominance of this area is not wholly embraced. A photograph by Mike Seaborne in the Museum of London archive neatly expresses some of the anger people felt at the imposition: at the junction of the Lea and City Mill Rivers, 'FUCK SEB CO [sic]' sprayed onto a pale green-grey packhorse bridge.[15]

The mania of the sporting event long gone, the left-behind landscape is entirely altered. What came before has been comprehensively erased – the allotments, the dog track, the silty tides, the marooned boats. Mad old London running to the wild. We are a city that easily forgets.

Robert Macfarlane recorded some of the 'many impro-vised ecologies – human and natural' that thrived in this region in a review of *Archaeology in Reverse* by Stephen Gill. His article was written in late 2007 and researched by stalking around the perimeter fence with Iain Sinclair.[16] Both men's sense of loss is underlined by the example of Manor Gardens Allotments. Macfarlane writes that 'all allotments are beautifully chronic places: developed over time, cobbled lovingly into being'. He explains that until very recently 80 plots at Manor Gardens provided food for more than 150 families during the summer months, as well as being 'superbly biodiverse'. Despite their social and nat-ural value, the allotments were locked away behind the big blue fence and bulldozed a few weeks later.

Today, the stadium and its cohorts sit on the island cre-ated by the Lee Navigation and the City Mill River, with the true River Lea running through the middle. For now the Olympic Park is a construction site, populated pre-dominantly by men in high-vis and hard hats, and private security guards in black patrol cars. And by shoppers. That giant mall looms over everything, drawing in huge num-bers of visitors every day. Come to Stratford and breathe the freshly conditioned air.

It's not all bad, in fact much of the wildlife habitat being created to replace what's been lost should be good.

There's promise of 2,000 trees and 350,000 wetland plants, as well as frog ponds, otter holts and kingfisher banks.[17] And Londoners have a huge new park to play in. The landscaping has been done with nature, walkers and cyclists in mind. There are soft-edged riverbanks for marginal plants and the birds and insects they support, and wider, resurfaced towpaths. New water controls, rubbish clearance and dredging work should, in theory, make the Back Rivers easier to navigate, if and when they fully reopen to boats.[18]

What I dislike about it all is the overwhelmingly corporate feel of the new world order that's being created. This is T.S. Eliot's unreal city circa 2014, the new faceless face of London. Every big project – see also Crossrail's squeeze on Soho in town – is an excuse to cleanse and to homogenise. Sweeping development is rarely nuanced, and nothing is allowed to be lovingly improvised, chronic or cobbled. In its wake, water often becomes a passive thing, decorative detail. How it functions is not as important as how it looks. People who voice their opposition, who ask if there is another way things can be done, are dismissed as crackpots or nimbys ('not in my back yard'). The new city veneer is one that is painstakingly designed and carefully controlled; genius loci is laid waste.

I take a walk in the park with animator and theatre-maker

Paul, who has watched London's big project take shape over the last seven years from his studio high up in Hackney Wick. I ask to meet him after watching his theatre company 1927's play *Golem*, which graphically illustrates what happens when we give up personal liberty and local identity for material comfort and an ostensibly easier life.

The play centres around a brother and sister, Robert and Annie – who were abandoned at a young age by their hedonistic parents – and their grandmother. She has brought the children up on a diet of Beethoven and anarchy; television is strictly banned. Now adults, Robert is a nerd and Annie is a punk. One evening Robert buys a golem from an inventor friend. In Jewish folklore a golem is an animated being created from inanimate matter. It obeys your every command, thinks what you think, does what you say. In 1927's play, Robert's golem begins benign but upgrades into something sinister. Rather than Robert controlling it, it controls Robert, while letting him think he is still in charge of his life. The family's eccentricities slowly erode as the golem's knowledge and influence grows. Around them, the quirky town where they live is taken over by chain stores. Life and landscape become deeply bland.

An undercurrent of horror at the commercialisation of modern life runs right through *Golem*, as it explores how we have given up our liberty to corporations that we know very little about. The spirit of Edward Snowden quietly haunts it. It's a wildly and wonderfully visual play that's ultimately about being blind.

There's an interview with Paul in the show's programme in which he reveals some of the places that shaped his designs for *Golem*'s animated set. London was a major influence, and specifically this territory between the rivers at Hackney Wick:

> I have watched the Olympic village being built literally across the river from my studio. This is undoubtedly one of the most pronounced visions of the corporate future to be seen in Europe. It was developed from a wonderful wasteland upon which all kinds of life thrived, both human and animal, into a desolate space.[19]

As Paul and I tour about the park on foot, our bemusement grows. We tie ourselves in knots trying to make sense of it. An article in *Property Week* from 2003 quotes the then director of the London Development Agency, Tony Winterbottom, saying that the central, public zone of the Olympic area would have 'a bit of a Disney feel to it'.[20] Post-Games, it still does, in a hollowed-out sort of way.

The landscape is masterplanned and sculpted; it is also disorientating and empty. Wide avenues, odd icons, blank spaces. As we walk, we deflate. Paul describes the dramatic changes that have been wrought here, concluding that, as Londoners, we are so used to transformations that we have come to expect beloved things to disappear and be replaced overnight. Nothing is sacrosanct, nothing is stable. How can we resist change in London when London is change itself? This city is unrecognisable from one decade to the next, from one year to the next. We have chosen to live in a place of flux; a city that inspires and excites but also alienates. I think about my London friends and how manic and unsettled we all often feel.

As Paul and I continue to explore, we begin to worry about our cynicism; London does need more homes after all. But does she need more expensive ones? The proportion of housing in the Olympic Park that will be 'affordable' could be as low as 15 per cent, according to a recent article in the *Hackney Gazette*.[21] Who knows what would have happened to this island on the outer edge of London had it been left to its own devices, but Paul predicts people would have eventually changed it from within, albeit in a more haphazard and slapdash way. It would have seen the kind of organic regeneration that gradually takes hold of a place and sees it self-transform; the kind of growth that is motivated by need and desire, and doesn't rely on Compulsory Purchase Orders and evictions. On the other side of the Lee Navigation – here the waterway is the dividing line between two distinct worlds – Hackney Wick has reinvented itself over several years. It has done it messily, joyfully, democratically, and without following a single narrative decreed from on high. The Wick's is not an imposed vision, or it hasn't been up to now. The developers have started to take note.

For the Bow Back Rivers, the Olympic project has had a considerable ecological cost: the new Three Mills Lock has stolen their tide. The rivers may look neater and tidier but the water is more vulnerable than it was before. That pollution incident in summer 2013 – the one where oxygen levels in the River Lea plummeted and thousands of fish died – was likely made worse because of the effects of the new lock. Without the agitation of rising and falling tides, the river water above the lock is now more susceptible to dissolved oxygen crashes. Pollution incidents in the Lea are not uncommon but before the new lock was installed the impact on the fish population didn't appear to be so dire. Post-Olympics, the Lea running through the park no longer functions properly as a river system. It will be interesting to hear what the European Commission's Water

Framework Directive inspectors make of the new lock; so far they haven't been able to assess its impact.[22]

Why exactly are the Back Rivers no longer tidal? In an interview with the *Guardian* in 2009, a senior Environment Agency officer said there were 'concerns that the duckweed won't look good in aerial photographs of the Olympic site at Stratford. Everyone is looking at Stratford now. It is a big driver for change'.[23] A throw-away comment about pondweed perhaps, but revealing too. It highlights just how important the aesthetics of London's big project was. The new Three Mills Lock means the water level in the Back Rivers is kept consistent throughout the park. It's not hard to imagine that mud banks and the gulls they attract could have been considered an eyesore, and, like duckweed, something to be avoided in those aerial shots.

The expense of installing the new lock was primarily justified, however, as a way of encouraging sustainable transport. It would allow 250,000 tonnes of concrete, gravel, sand and stone to arrive at the construction site by boat, taking a significant number of lorries off the roads. This sounds positive but barely any building materials were shipped in this way. After the lock opened in June 2009, 600 tonnes of aggregate were transported to the site by water over the rest of that year, the equivalent of just two large barge loads.[24] An Aggregates Industry case study showcasing its work on the Olympic Park fails to provide any information about the quantity of building materials brought in by barge, reporting instead that the 'majority of aggregate materials have been delivered to the Olympic Park by rail'.[25] And in its assessment of logistics during the Games themselves, the Commission for a Sustainable London 2012 reports that only 'two limited trials of barging material were undertaken under different operating conditions from Tilbury to docks at Tower Hamlets'.[26] It seems that cosmetics could well be the real reason the rivers lost their tide, at great public expense, that and the brief thrill of David Beckham arriving at the opening ceremony by speedboat.[27]

The past is being rewritten, rejected even. Those involved with the Olympics insist the Back Rivers were barren and inaccessible before they came along and opened them up. Talk to people who walked along the waterways before 2007 – there were paths and self-guided walks, maintained and publicised in leaflets by the no-longer-operating Lower Lea Project[28] – and you'll hear stories of incredible feats of fly-tipping, yes, but also of an area that was gloriously wild, and a River Lea that was tidal up to Hackney Wick and ecologically stronger as a result.

According to the government, £50 million has been spent by various agencies on the waterways here.[29] From the perspective of a continuously cruising boater, the new water controls should open up more territory for us to explore and moor in. This would be welcome. London's boating community is growing apace, and the housing crisis that's pushing more and more people onto the water shows no sign of easing. There is an urgent need for more facilities for boaters who live and work in London, and for more fourteen-day mooring spaces where we can park our boats. However, the fear is that the Back Rivers will eventually reopen improved for navigation but with strict new rules in place and catering primarily for tourists.

The Lee Navigation is wide here at Hackney Wick where it meets the Hertford Union, a two-kilometre canal that allows boaters a shortcut up three locks to join the Regent's Canal at Victoria Park. Continuing south along the Lee, the industrial-artistic district known as Fish Island is on the right and the Olympic Park development extends down to the towpath on the left. The bank is busy with boats. There's a precious water tap and black waste disposal point at Old Ford Lock. Beyond the mechanised lock – which you operate with a key and a button, rather than a windlass and elbow grease – are some reed beds (something the Lee Navigation generally lacks), several brand new blocks of flats, a set of heavily decorated old waterside warehouses and a community of particularly bohemian-looking boats. The Lee changes dramatically after this point. The vigour and enterprise of the north is lost, and the Navigation becomes austere. It passes low down, underused and unloved, caged inside hoardings. What little vegetation there is is caked in grey dust from nearby construction sites. Roads and rail tracks criss-cross overhead, boxing the river in and blocking out the sky.

After filling up with water at Old Ford, we cruise down-river. A cormorant emerges from a dive, unexpected and out of nowhere, inside one of the bare rooms created by the angular undersides of the road bridges. The bird appears in silhouette, a shadow sliding under and over water the colour of concrete. Light moves through the low-ceilinged rooms in hazy shafts, picking out floating particles of dirt and dust.

After this desolate stretch, Three Mills is a surprising sight. The old tidal mill once distilled gin and ground flour; it's now a film studio. It sits between the Lee Navigation and the River Lea proper, whose confusion of channels have now escaped the Olympic Park and are neatly reu-nited in the tidal Bow Creek. The canal boats are back on the Navigation, mooring in the wake of the red-brick relic. This building is a reminder of how important the Back

Rivers once were to industry, powering the various mills that rose up along their banks. Three Mills is the only one left. Even it didn't quite escape the Olympics. Once a thriving independent studio, it gave in to intense pressure and was sold to the London Development Agency in 2004, then used to plan the opening, closing and victory ceremonies for the Olympic and Paralympic Games.[30] TV shows and films are still made here but it is now owned by the London Legacy Development Corporation.

Far wider-reaching changes are afoot. Three new housing developments are being built around the rivers, one masterminded by Ikea,[31] one by Tesco, one by East Thames/Southern Housing.[32] A new Bow Lock School will open in the autumn, with windows that don't open on the A12 side because of the traffic fumes. Maps showing the reach of the Ikea development – called Strand East – which will be commercial as well as residential, shows it extending all along the waterways, but it's unclear whether cruising boats will still be able to moor up. The Strand East website does mention 'boats selling books, beer or bric-a-brac', a list chosen for its alliterative qualities rather than having much real meaning, I suspect.[33] As London grows upwards and outwards and ever more sleek, the opportunities for cruisers to moor threaten to shrink.

For now, the area around Three Mills and down to Bow

Lock remains a lonely, isolated spot with its own appeal and several casual moorings. The tide's out creekside and Canada geese group together in the silty intertidal shallows. One is leucistic – instead of a black face and bill, with smart white chin strap, this bird has a scruffy white face and a yellow bill with a wide band of pink at the tip. A lone grey heron preens in the mud. Black-headed gulls gather. We are reaching the Lee's end.

At Bow Lock, boats can join the Limehouse Cut, a poker-straight channel that runs west to the old Regent's Canal Dock, now Limehouse Basin. Bow Creek winds its way down to the Thames at East India Dock. Before splitting up for good, the Navigation and Creek run side by side for a time, the towpath balanced on a spit between the two. The concrete bridge that directs foot traffic off the spit and away from the Creek is covered all over with big bright spots of yellow lichen, *Xanthoria parietina.* There's been a lock of sorts here for hundreds of years but water used to flow over the top of the gates at high tide.[34] New gates were fitted in 2000, which has made the Cut and the Navigation, both previously semi-tidal and brackish, totally tide-free.[35] Before that both navigations were silting up and the Limehouse towpath regularly used to flood, which meant pedestrian access had to be limited. Controlling man-made watercourses for practical reasons like this makes sense; stealing a natural river's cleansing tides seems far less justifiable.

The Limehouse Cut was built in 1770. When it was still a working canal, its waters were apparently 'so noxious that it was said that no bargee who fell in had any chance of surviving'.[36] Polluting businesses on the canal banks included potash, quicklime and chemical factories. Originally it cut through countryside but the waterway was a catalyst and the rural environs quickly transformed into the dense, industrial districts of Poplar and Limehouse.[37] The canal here hasn't completely thrown off its insalubrious shades but it is no longer deadly. At its eastern end the waterway is edged by modern light industry and old brick warehouses, further west by blocks of flats. Built up along its entire route, it's a dark and tunnel-like passage. It's not a desert though. Gulls line up single file on warehouse roofs, each beak pointing north-west, each tail turned Thames-ward. A cormorant joins their ranks but faces the other way. Three pure white ducks sleep soundly on a floating, purpose-built platform. Amid the brick and corrugation, a pair of great crested grebes cut a dash. Buddleia sprouts in energetic bursts from the walls and the path.

The short canal ends at Limehouse Basin. Commercial operations ended here in 1969 and it was redeveloped along with the rest of the Docklands in the eighties. Most of the wharves and warehouses were demolished, new flats went up and a modern marina was established. It has room for around 90 boats, ranging from humble canal barges to flashy yachts and giant sailing ships. DLR trains pass overhead, a link road tunnels underneath, the Thames is close at hand. There's something coastal about this place; there's a whiff of sea salt in the air. At the top of the basin, through a ship lock, the Regent's Canal begins its journey north then west to Little Venice. It's where true artifice begins.

spring

—◆—

wasteland

Regent's Canal

Victoria Park
to Rosemary Branch

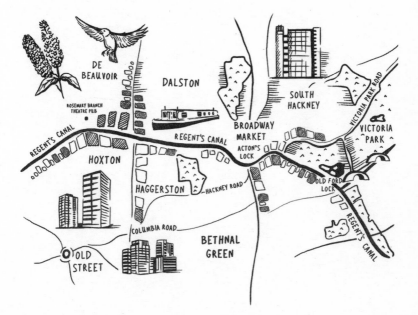

6. the cut

The Regent's Canal is a hairline fracture along London's x-axis; a thin fissure in a valley of brick, glass and stone. It's a landscape you descend into where turbid waters pool rather than flow. An obstinate geographical fact, the canal-scape has recently been reimagined as footpath, cycleway and running track, as nature reserve, boat park and estate agent's wet dream. Most of us are drawn to water and, in a city, even a shallow concrete channel, a mere moat, can have irresistible appeal.

We have learned to call the canal 'the Cut'. It's a name that expresses its slim shape, its depth, its certain tang. It also invokes the past. This industrial gash, this wet wound, was sliced into the earth by hand. It may have more in common with a pond than a river, but the water's character is mobile. Sometimes the Cut is stretched out smooth and tight, a high-sheen sheet of smoked glass; other times it is sharply crumpled; others gently ribbed and ruffed. It's moulded into shade and shape by the weather, and the creatures and boats that move through it. It is a chameleon, a waterway with what Ted Hughes might call a 'picture-skin', one that absorbs and reflects back all that is around and above it.[38]

I would walk the towpath before I lived on a boat but my feelings about it didn't helter-skelter as they do now, sharpening because my fortunes are bound up within it. The landscape surprises me most days. It's such a shape-shifter. A Jekyll and a Hyde. A fixed line that is grim in places, inviting in others, slipping from hostile to benign, from romantic to weird, and back. All cities need something like it, something old and imperfect, littered but alive, an attractor of strange fowl and folk. The Cut is another volatile place then, another fault line along which to make a home.

Spring breaks. The ceaseless wind and rain of the last few months passes to leave warm sunshine and blue skies. Puddles evaporate at long last. It's still cool enough to light the fire in the evenings but in the mornings we are brave enough to do without. We are now moored at Victoria Park in the skeletal canopy of leafless park planes, the last boat in a long line and beside a powder-blue and brick-red footbridge. Along the towpath, low growth is brightly dotted with buttery yellow celandines and royal blue green alkanet. Fresh graffiti glistens in the sun, acid orange paint drip-dripping off walls and onto new blades of grass.

I'm inside the boat spying on S. He is outside, sitting on the front deck smoking, sunlit and thoughtful, his face full of things I'll never know. I watch the glow and the crackle of the draw on his lips, the controlled exhalation, the dirty yellow curls as they float away. It's a seductive scene: him and his unknowable thoughts, framed by the pretty brick bridge behind, which itself is caught up by the still-bare trees just in bud. All this reflects and doubles in the flat mirror surface of the water. I battle the urge to interrupt, to insert myself, and instead turn to look out of the kitchen window.

The stream of knees, calves and feet loping past has steadily increased as the new season takes hold. The park will surely be busier today than it has been in months. The filmstrip view through the slatted blind presents flickering shots of blackbirds, parakeets and squirrels as well as wheels, shoes and dogs. The towpath is narrow here, concrete from the water's edge back to a strip of earth and low-growing plants, then railings, shrubs and the park, where cherry trees and daffodils bloom. People pass by within inches of the boat; if I could reach out through the glass we'd be able to touch.

The topography of this part of the Regent's Canal is

both typical and atypical. Typical, first, because it follows a prescribed pattern. The cross section begins with a barrier (railings, a wall or a building) running alongside a towpath verge (a thin strip of earth and plants) that in turn runs alongside the towpath (the paved walkway). This, of course, runs beside the waterway itself. On the other side of the water – the off side – there is another barrier, then the city beyond. It's also typical because street level is a good few feet above water level, and on a boat or the towpath you can be looked down upon from a bridge.

It's atypical because beyond the towpath verge and its barrier is a park. Over its eight-and-a-half-mile route from Limehouse to Little Venice, the Regent's Canal runs past parkland at Mile End and Regent's Park as well as here, but generally it is built up, bordered on both sides by residential and commercial buildings. It varies across its course, but the waterway is about 40 to 60 feet wide, with a navigational depth of around four feet. It has a gentle incline, rising 85 feet via twelve locks, and the towpath is generally wide enough for two, now imaginary, horses to pass. The offside edges are occasionally silty and soft enough to support marginal plants.

When compared to the River Thames, the canal is not only fake, it's also tame. Nobody is ever going to convincingly assert that these sluggish waters represent the lifeblood of the city. But the Thames most of us experience day-to-day is encased inside high concrete banks and caged behind walls and rails. It has few natural-feeling features on its journey through London's central parts, and most of us view it from a high-up, disconnected distance. The canal may be smaller in scale and entirely artificial in origin, with none of the myth and legend the River has long inspired, but it is far more accessible. It too is concreted in but it is a waterway you can actually walk right alongside, even touch. Spending time beside it or on it is a modest experience when compared with a trip down the Thames but the canal has an allure that cannot be dismissed. The crowds of people that walk, cycle, run and boat along it every day testify to that.

In the last few years, and for various reasons, the canal has become a domestic space as much as a recreational one. There have been people living on the water in London for decades but there's no denying that the boating community has ballooned dramatically of late, a direct consequence of outrageous property prices on land. In a city where a shoebox of a one-bedroom flat averages over £300,000, and where rent is unregulated, it's no real surprise that the capital's waterways are getting busier. Becoming a live-aboard boater is not necessarily cheap – you have to buy a boat for a start, then there's the annual licence fee, insurance, fuel and upkeep costs – but if you want a place of your own, free of the tyranny of letting agents and landlords, it can be a viable alternative for some people.

A significant proportion of the Cut, although by no means all of it, is lined with boats, sometimes two or even three abreast, usually on the towpath side. London's canals are wide – because the barges that used them traditionally were wide – and so the waterway can be three boats deep in places and still perfectly navigable. Live-aboard narrowboats of all lengths share the water with homes fashioned out of broad-shouldered wide beams, sporty plastic cruisers, converted Norwegian lifeboats and picturesque Dutch barges with anchors, wheelhouses and masts. There's an infamous inflatable with a tent on top and a floating garden shed. Some boats only the goodwill of the water gods keeps afloat.

We probably all nurse a mental image of how a classic canal boat should look but contemporary ones follow no rules when it comes to exterior decoration. Harlequin diamonds and fancy rope-work seem to be on the wane but the mysterious rose and castle motif is proving more durable. Traditional designs most often decorate the pristine boats of the seasonal cruisers who pass through in slow pursuit of an adventure on the Thames. London's live-aboard boats are a motlier crew. Sleek new ones, brash and bullish, moor alongside scrappy rust buckets. Some vessels are plain and apparently nameless, others sport hand-painted murals. Names are displayed in typographic styles ranging from circus-style block caps through elaborate baroque to sans serif sleek and felt-tip pen on paper, Blu-Tacked to the window. There's a narrowboat with a jaw of bright gummy teeth spray-painted all down the side; another sports a life-size, tattoo-like hula girl. You can guess at how long someone has been on the Cut by the amount of stuff on the boat's roof. Some are clear, but many are chaotic with plants, palettes, wood, coal, rotting furniture and maybe an accident-prone cat.

In this few metres between two bridges at Victoria Park, several live-aboard boats are moored nose to rear deck in a long row along the towpath, parked for a fortnight each. It's the most interesting of all streets, no two homes the same, each residence with its own quirks, and the make-up and order of things fluid. Here uniformity is wholly rejected in favour of difference. A small, boxy blue and red narrowboat with variegated ivy growing round the door nudges next to a huge wide beam that is painted the palest of pinks and faintly gleams like the inside of a shell. The husk of a white cruiser, tight wrapped with tarpaulins, a boat-shaped gift, sits beside a long black narrowboat, gothic with its heavily leaded windows and etched pinhole portholes. A handsome Dutch barge, painted glossy cream and chocolate brown, with a wheelhouse hung about with hurricane lamps, is neighbours with a Spartan-looking narrowboat without curtains and still naked in its grey primer. Each roof is differently stacked, each deck a different shape. One vessel has a long, distinguished Greek god of a nose, one a stubby, wide snout, another looks distinctly sharkish. Across the water is a small private, residential mooring, with a rainbow of bunting and a garden shed.

It's impossible to generalise about who we all are other than to say we are as mixed a bunch as you would find on land: families, couples, students, retirees, professionals, artists, dreamers, depressives. Boating tribes include newbies, old hands, hobbyists, tourists and lone wolves. The disparateness of our lives and our approaches means the sense of community can be weak as well as strong. There are business boats moored along with residential ones, although, beyond the fuel barges, these don't cater for boaters per se. The proprietors are keen to attract passing towpath trade, positioning themselves in the spots where people are most drawn to the canal. There are several cafés, a boutique, two theatres, a vinyl stall and a bookshop, and floating office, studio and classroom space for hire. London's canals have become linear villages; dynamic, travelling townscapes that are eclectic, textured and always shifting about. Who is where isn't fixed, and one week will be different from the next. Boaters make up a tiny fraction of the city's 8 million inhabitants, but we're an increasing minority that river authorities and local councils are well aware of. If you live near a towpath or use one to commute, we're hard to miss.

— ◆◆◆ —

For me, the decision to buy a boat was practical and emotional. After ten long years renting rooms in cramped shared flats, I craved space, change and a genuine home with only my loved ones in it. We can partly blame the urgent need for stability and stimulation on turning 30. A new decade demands a new approach. Buying bricks is a far wiser investment, but self-employed low-earners don't get mortgages easily and flats in London, as we know, are overpriced. It's easy for someone who can't get a loan to say, but surely there has to be a point when we refuse to pay hundreds of thousands of pounds for a few square feet of shelter. In protest, perhaps we should stop crippling ourselves with debt and instead invest in living in ways that feel sustainable, in the widest sense, not least economically.

A canal boat we could live on permanently was something S. and I had long daydreamed of and researched heavily. It wasn't just about money. It was about having a new relationship with London, and with each other. If we lived on a boat we believed we would have more control over our lives and our impact; we could attempt to live off-grid, we could simplify things, strip back. We could have solar panels.

I decided to lodge with a friend of a friend on their narrowboat for a while to learn the ropes. It was an eventful few weeks during an abnormally cold March. My berth was also the corridor between the bathroom and the living cabin; I slept with a hot water bottle and cocooned inside three sleeping bags, always wearing a woolly jumper and a pair of thick socks. I made my first fire and gradually earned my sea legs, after feeling knock-kneed for days. I dropped my keys and my bike lock in the river; only the bike lock was fished out. I learned that a strong magnet and a boat hook are important tools for boaters with butter fingers. I experienced my first cassette chemical loo and the process of disposing of the stewing shit, manually. We cruised north, then east. I mastered my first lock. The boat broke down under an unsavoury road bridge, just after we rescued a sodden and motherless mallard duckling by catching it in a saucepan. It perked up considerably for a time before dropping dead. Our hearts were left as broken as the engine. The whole experience was surreal and I was convinced. It was time to act.

You buy a boat outright rather than relying on a mortgage and so you need capital to do it. Boats with residential moorings in London are exceptionally rare and generally expensive so we decided to forgo that luxury, planning to cruise rather than moor permanently in one place. We hunted Pike down in Derbyshire, and then spent all the money and energy we had making her ours. Getting her to London – by road and by river – was a feat. But, by clubbing together and buying her outright, S. and I gained the security of a decent place of our own to call home and exited the rental market with relief.

7. flora, fauna

A place where rough, ruderal land meets torpid water has potency, and the mixing up of the wet and the dry along the Regent's Canal means it can support much wild as well as human life. For me, the Cut's flora and fauna are an attraction, a distraction and a source of reassurance. It's not just about aesthetics. Artificial waterways are part of our ecosystem; in fact they have become increasingly important 'natural' features as traditional ponds have disappeared. The London Biodiversity Partnership (LBP) says 'open standing water represents one of the most diverse of all ecological habitats' and describes the city's canal network specifically as an 'asset for nature conservation'. LBP also explains that canals and ditches 'will be increasingly important to build species resilience against climate change'.[39]

The whole of London's canal system was designated a Site of Importance for Nature Conservation (SINC) in 1986, after a comprehensive survey of its wildlife was carried out. The SINC citation states that 'London's network of canals

fulfil an important function in allowing nature into heavily built-up environments', listing the many aquatic and
waterside plants, invertebrates, fish and breeding waterfowl that the city's canals were then found to support.

I ask Greenspace Information for Greater London
(GiGL) – the capital's environmental records centre – to
do an ecological data search into London's navigable waterways, excluding the Thames. GiGL dive into their vast data
pool and emerge with 33,841 wildlife records, dating from
1970 to the present day, and relating to a focus area that
covers the Regent's Canal, the London sections of the Grand
Union north to Uxbridge and south to Brentford, the canal
feeder channels, the Hertford Union, the Limehouse Cut
and the Lee Navigation from Bow Lock up to Springfield
Marina. Most are records of flowering plants, birds and
insects but there are numerous sightings of bats as well.
The twenty most recorded taxa over that 45-year period,
with the most recorded first, are:

- Blackbird
- Woodpigeon
- Robin
- Jackdaw
- Pipistrelle bat
- Wren

- Blue tit
- Ash
- Small white butterfly
- Magpie
- Buddleia
- Common nettle
- Great tit
- Bramble
- Speckled wood butterfly
- Green veined white butterfly
- Hawthorn
- Sycamore
- Perennial rye-grass
- Elder

Some of the more interesting records that the data search pulls up include rarities for London like tawny owl, cinnabar moth, grass snake and stag beetle on or close to the Grand Union north to Uxbridge; water vole, fieldfare, red kite and great crested newt on or around the Paddington Branch; honey-buzzard, skylark, pennyroyal and brown-banded carder bee on or close to the Regent's Canal; kingfisher and spotted flycatcher on or around the Limehouse Cut; and Arctic tern, curlew, marsh harrier, merlin, osprey, ring ouzel and spotted crake in close vicinity of the Lee. The data shows that all the waterways support a variety of bat species including Daubenton's, Nathusius', Natterer's, noctule and soprano pipistrelle. Most astounding of all is that European otter has been sighted on both the Regent's Canal and the Lee Navigation as recently as 2013.

It's exciting to think of all of these creatures existing here, but it would be disingenuous to suggest London's navigations are in any way perfect refuges for wildlife. There needs to be another in-depth survey of the network, one that accurately assesses the ecological state of things today. I believe if we were able to directly compare the 1980s survey with a new one, we would likely have to acknowledge that, as the waterways' popularity has grown, their wildness has decreased. An urban canal is a tough environment, where wildlife faces a host of pressures, and plants, birds, animals and insects are in constant competition over limited resources. As more people are attracted to the water, for whatever reasons, the pressure on nature here will only increase unless the space is managed differently.

Richard Mabey considers the importance and also the fragility of the urban canal as habitat in *The Unofficial Countryside*, describing the 'nightmarishly complex web of forces' at play in a pond-like place that is often expected to behave like a river. He highlights how little the water moves, describing the 'paltry cleansing action the sluicing of the locks provides' and how 'an untended canal will be choked with mud and weed after very few years'. Mabey goes on to debate the double-edged role that moving boats, which have a scouring action, play in this precarious ecosystem: vessels break up weed and keep silt mobile, but they also cause bank erosion.

There are many more boats in London today than there were when Mabey wrote his ode to urban nature in the 1970s, especially on the Regent's Canal. The increasing number of people living here means it is far less of a sleepy backwater than it was during its days of abandonment. More boats mean more disturbance and less aquatic and marginal vegetation, but also more movement and in turn more scouring, flushing and induced flow. The canal's water quality is surprisingly good. You'd be a fool to drink it, or even swim in it, but the presence of fish and fish-eaters like cormorants, herring gulls and grey herons proves that the Regent's is relatively clean. That said, motor boats do have an impact and are no doubt responsible for some water pollution: anything diesel- or petrol-powered is dirty.

The Cut's growing popularity, with people on foot and on bicycles as much as on boats, is its vulnerability.

As towpath traffic increases, so does the amount of litter gathering under bridges, around weirs and at locks. The problem must be worse now we are a nation of takeaway coffee drinkers who find it hard to go anywhere without something disposable clasped in our phone-free hand. And people dump worse things than that – scooters, bikes, shopping baskets, body parts. Murder victims have been ineffectively disposed of in the shallow Regent's Canal since it opened, but perhaps the grimmest discovery of all was made in 2010, when the severed head of an actress was found in the canal in east London.[40] Mostly people dump supermarket trolleys. In a single year, more than 3,000 trolleys were hauled out of the UK's rivers and canals.[41] Waterways have long been repositories for the unwanted and the incriminatory, and the underwater landscape, when glimpsed, is one rocky with discarded debris.

I am biased, but as a live-aboard boater I think the positive impact our community has outweighs any negatives. It is often boaters who feel most compelled to haul rubbish out of the Cut, after all. The Regent's Canal is not a sterile place, and in many ways it is the imperfections that make it interesting. It is possible to enjoy the coupling of the natural and the man-made – the dewy little mound of moss clinging to the concrete towpath edge, the steel houseboat bobbing on the wind-brushed water, even the coot building a magnificent plastic bag and bottle nest. The litter troubles me, but the fact a cormorant can ignore it and continue to fish gives me hope.

As a Londoner living in a crowded city, on an entirely artificial water strip, I believe human beings are as fundamental a part of the canal-scape as the birds, the plants and the fish. It was people after all, the local ones who recognised its amenity and natural value, who ensured the Cut as we now know it survived.

In 1967, a visionary report was published that dared to imagine a future for the canal that didn't involve infilling it and turning it into a road, which was then being seriously proposed. *The Regent's Canal – A Policy For Its Future* was the product of two years' work, and describes the canal's history and qualities, as well as setting out a compelling argument as to how and why the waterway could become 'a major feature of great attraction in north London'. For the authors, the canal was a 'problematic physical feature' but one that might be transformed in 'the new age of leisure'.

Back then the Regent's Canal was hidden from view, neglected and closed off. It had been nationalised in 1948, but the towpath wasn't a public right of way and you could only use it if you had a permit. There were hardly any boats on the water, and possibly as few as 31 residential ones. Commercial carrying did still take place, and twelve tractor-drawn barges were daily shifting goods up and down the eastern part of the Regent's Canal and Hertford Union. Short-haul cargo was mainly timber but also included marble and paper. Further west, an average of just one boat a day was passing through City Lock in Angel. London's locks were still operated by lock-keepers who kept strict hours. The canal, both waterway and adjacent path, was an awkward, hard-to-use space.

The report explains that 'with the decline of water traffic the canal has become a neglected backwater. It runs through parts of London notably deficient in open space and generally of low environmental quality, but does little to offset these characteristics'. It goes on to describe the floating rubbish that accumulates on bends and above locks, the bikes and prams that have sunk to the bottom, and the kids who like to throw stones or fire airguns at passing boats.

Despite all this, the authors look at the stagnant ditch running close to their homes and daydream of Amsterdam and Venice. They celebrate the Cut's 'infinite variety', its 'rapid changes of scene', the way it links 'in a panorama all aspects of the city's life from gracious living to heavy industry'. They assert, persuasively, that 'beneath the grime and dereliction the landscape of the canal has a distinct and fascinating character', and that it's 'not necessary to rationalise the various ways in which water affects its setting and vice versa; we all know by sight and sound its unique qualities'. The report's authors had imagination, passion and influence, and they helped save the Regent's Canal.

The plans for a road were scrapped and, while kids certainly do still throw stones and, today, fireworks at passing boats and all kinds of rubbish still floats on the surface and sits on the bottom, the canal has been transformed in the way those 1960s visionaries hoped it would. It has taken time but the towpath is now open to all and generally well used, and the waterway is once again busy with boats. Although not as wild as it once was, today it contributes a huge amount to the urban landscape, a genuine compensation in inner-city areas that otherwise lack green space.

— ◆◆◆ —

In her current spot at Victoria Park, Pike is moored inside a triangle marked out by three singing bushes. One is east of here at the intersection between the Hertford Union and the Regent's Canal, another overspills from a private garden onto the towpath close to Mare Street. The most vocal is on the offside bank, just west of Victoria Park and in front of an old brick warehouse. This particular bush is the largest canal-side buddleia I know of in London. It is 55 paces long – almost twice the length of Pike – and I guess three metres high and two metres thick. The noise all three bushes emit is incredible; they whistle and sing and chirrup and chatter. It takes a while to decipher the source of the music but if you look into them for long enough you'll start to pick out the dark shapes of the house sparrows, and notice their small forms darting across the water between the shrubs.

W.H. Hudson's 1898 book *Birds in London* documents the natural state of things when the capital's canal network was still fulfilling its original purpose. It surveys the avifauna the city supported back then, and sketches out the wider landscape. Hudson isn't especially positive about Victoria Park, which was around 50 years old when he wrote, and habitually blanketed in smoke. His disdain extends to his description of its shape as 'like a somewhat gouty or swollen leg and foot, the leg cut off below the knee'. He knew the canal–park combination had potential though, and wrote admiringly of the Cut as it passed through Regent's Park, explaining it was 'along the canal where birds are always most abundant, and where the finest melody may be heard'. I think Hudson might be pleasantly surprised at how Victoria Park and the canal alongside it have evolved.

When Hudson wrote, sparrows were common, 'intimately known to every man, woman, and child in the metropolis, even to the meanest gutter child in the poorest district'. He describes 'daily gatherings of a pacific nature at some favourite meeting-place', where a chorus of rude music would ring out, and explains that these meeting places were then known to Londoners as sparrows' chapels. In contrast, at the turn of the last century, the gregarious bird's predominance had waned considerably. Once on a par with feral pigeons for ubiquity – and so much a part of daily life that they were recognised in Cockney slang as the bow and arrow – three quarters of London's house sparrow population was lost between 1994 and 2000.[42] Lack of habitat is one factor blamed for the species' decline, so these canal-side chapels at Victoria Park are bastions of sorts.

Hudson's sparrows didn't gather in buddleia bushes. The self-seeding shrub was first brought over from China in the decade when he was writing but it didn't go rogue in Britain until after the Second World War, when it rushed through bomb sites, revelling in all the exposed rubble and ruin. Today it's London's most tenacious shrub, one that offers nectar and shelter to small creatures in otherwise inhospitable areas. I've always admired its brazen ways – the way it rampages through urban areas and clings to the side of buildings. A city chimney in 2014 is far more likely to sport a plume of bush than smoke. With its terrain of old brick warehouses, walls, bridges and walkways, the Regent's Canal mimics buddleia's natural habitat of rocky mountaintops and dry shingle, and it is one of the Cut's most common plants.

Buddleia is part of the canal's wall-and-crack flora, along with lichens, mosses, ferns and wildflowers like herb-Robert, bellflower and pellitory-of-the-wall. It's a community of plants that I'm drawn to, especially on the Cut's seemingly barren, most brutalist stretches, like the Regent's just west of here between Broadway Market and Kingsland Road. There is lots to see if you deign to crouch down and look. I carry a camera because I believe people will likely forgive a photographer for eccentric intimacies with the towpath. One day I'm sure someone will creep up behind and push me in.

Soft-tufted mounds of bright green wall-screw moss and grey-cushioned hedgehog moss hang on to the towpath's concrete edges and venture up its stone walls. More abundant than the mosses are the intricate frills of the so-called chewing gum lichen, *Lecanora muralis*, which leaves circular green-grey prints all over the towpath's walls and walkways. Even the benches are spattered with it. Its ragged polka dots could be mistaken for gull poo as much as gum, I think. It mixes up with the whiter barnacle-like swellings of *Lecanora sp.* and the very occasional ochre blister of *Candelariella sp.*

Before the invention of the microscope, lichens were believed to be plants, but strong magnification revealed them to be a symbiotic coupling of fungus and alga. The fungus acts as the body, providing the alga with protection, while the alga provides the fungus with food. Only if you peer at lichen in extreme close up will you witness its exquisite frills, blisters and swellings. Lichens absorb water, nutrients and pollutants across their entire surface, which means they act as excellent bioindicators and are useful for interpreting environmental change. Branched, stalked and bushy fruticose lichens have the greatest surface area of all and are only found in places with clean air. They abound in rural areas but are hard to find in London, although *Evernia prunastri* has been recorded in Regent's Park and *Usnea sp.* at Kew. The foliose and crustose lichens are more tolerant of urban conditions – *Hyperphyscia adglutinata*, the so-called pollution lichen for example, or *Lepraria*, a lichen able to tolerate acid rain. Alongside important, practical things like soil formation and absorbing carbon dioxide, lichens give a place a discreetly flocked texture, what Doris Lessing describes as 'minute animals' ears, a warm rough silk'.[43] With a hand lens, a dark brown skid on a paving slab is transformed into *Verrucania nigrescens* and a few spots of dust become *Lecidella stigmatea*.

I'm not a hunter of the rare or the exotic, I'm happy enough with buddleia, lichen, sparrows and moss, but I am nursing a desire to be able to identify more things. I arrange to meet Annie, a botanist and boater, at Victoria Park beside Old Ford Lock. (Confusingly, the Regent's Canal and the Lee Navigation each has its own Old Ford Lock.) We've never met before but it's easy to tell which figure is hers from a distance: the one with the rucksack and in walking boots, crouched close to the lock's edge and peering intently at something pushing out of the crack between two smooth bricks. Annie rises and we introduce ourselves, me explaining my desire to understand the towpath ecology better, my need to name.

Instantly generous with her knowledge, Annie reveals that her interest in plants first grew in this very place. Quite the pioneer, she would jog for long distances along the Regent's Canal towpath in the early 1980s, before it was claimed by the recreationalists and groomed into its current shape. Few people knew such things were possible back then and most days she had the Cut to herself. Untended, and only rarely disturbed by walkers and boats, the verges, walls and offside waste spaces had become riotous with plants. Running alone through this space, her blood pumping and mind racing, Annie's future course as an urban naturalist was set.

It's a different scene today, one Annie quietly recoils from. Too busy, too managed. Once the canal's amenity value had been affirmed and the mission to open it up rolled out in earnest, British Waterways determined to keep plants short and strimmed, soft patches were concreted over, and feet and wheels have since worn the vegetation closest to the towpath back to bare earth. Today canal land management in London appears mostly to be motivated by the neat and the tidy, although thankfully the use of chemical controls seems to have stopped. In earlier decades huge damage was done to the environment by dousing unwanted plants with pesticides that killed all and everything in their wake. Read Richard Mabey's account of the suspected poisoning of a young grey wagtail, after spraying close to the Grand Union Canal in west London, and weep.[44]

Despite her aversion to the Regent's Canal's current incarnation – Annie's much happier on the calmer and wilder River Lea, where she now lives on her boat – I easily persuade her to walk with me to Angel. We set out slowly west, our gaze cast low along the sparse verges, picking out whatever plants we see. It's the last day of March, gusty, sunny and cool. The early wildflowers and tree blossom are in bloom, but most of the plants are still young and only just emerging. There are very few flowers to ease our identification but encyclopaedic Annie knows her stuff and can work from leaves alone. We crouch, finger and sniff, carefully ignoring the dog poo and focusing on the green. Annie calls out plant names and I make notes, my fingers whitening in the numbing north-north-westerlies. Combing the towpath between Victoria Park and the Islington tunnel, we see:

* Adria bellflower
* Alexanders
* Alfalfa (lucerne)
* Annual mercury
* Black horehound (stinking Roger)
* Black knapweed
* Blackthorn
* Bracken
* Broad leaved dock
* Burclover (spotted medick)
* Burdock
* Caper spurge
* Chickweed
* Cleavers (sticky Willy)

- Common cat's-ear
- Common field speedwell (Veronica)
- Common mallow
- Common toadflax
- Cow parsley
- Crane's-bill
- Dandelion
- Eastern rocket
- Elder
- Evening primrose
- Fennel
- Great valerian
- Greek dock
- Green alkanet
- Ground ivy
- Groundsel
- Hedge mustard
- Hemlock
- Hemlock water dropwort
- Hoary cress
- Japanese honeysuckle
- Lesser celandine
- Lesser periwinkle
- Mugwort
- Mullein

- Pellitory-of-the-wall
- Petty spurge
- Prickly sow-thistle
- Red campion
- Red dead nettle
- Shepherd's purse
- Small nettle
- Sumatran fleabane
- Sweet violet
- Three-cornered leek
- White dead nettle
- Wood avens (herb Bennet)
- Yarrow
- Yellow corydalis
- Yellow sorrel

Ours is not a comprehensive list but it is a pleasingly long one, one that in the abstract gives the impression of verdure. That's not really the case. These plants exist in isolated snatches. Some are only eking out a living, just about surviving on the thinnest, dustiest scraps of dirt. With many you get the distinct feeling they are clinging on for dear life. But there are healthier, heartier clumps too – especially the hemlock, sweet violets and Alexanders – which give a glimpse of how good it could all surely be.

The Alexanders – also known as black lovage and as horse parsley – are a recent towpath colonist. The salt-tolerant plant is usually associated with clifftops and seaside paths but is making its way inland and thriving in a few places along the Regent's Canal. It was first introduced to Britain by the Romans, who called it the pot herb of Alexandria and cultivated it for use in salads and stews.[45] It's tall and bushy with greenish-yellow flowers and edible leaves, stems and seeds. It looks a bit like celery and can be used in the same way. My wildflower field guide calls Alexanders a 'gregarious plant' that is 'pungent when crushed'.[46] We duly crush it and release a herbal scent that recalls a heady, aromatic gin.

We see lots of hemlock with its red-spotted stems, dark leaves and mousy scent – foliage that Annie says speaks of its sinister nature – and one clump of hemlock water dropwort, which grows in the shallows and will later boast balls of white flowers. Both the hemlocks are wickedly poisonous. An online herbal has some good horror stories, describing an occasion when a group of workmen repairing a breach in a towing path dug up and ate the roots, mistaking them for parsnips. If only they'd known the roots of hemlock water dropwort are also known as dead man's fingers. Another work party picked hemlock leaves and added them to their cheese sandwiches as a relish. 'In each case death occurred within three hours,' according to the herbal, which reports a final incident where 'eight boys ate the roots, and five died – and the other three had violent convulsions and lost their reason for many hours'.[47]

I love a hair-raising tale about a plant's potency but let's not get carried away; the hemlocks' poisons are safely stored away in their roots and leaves and only do you harm if you are fool enough to eat them. Searching for more information about hemlock water dropwort, I find an entire web page devoted to its destruction on a well-known pesticide corporation's website. Monsanto reports the plant's potential dangers, labelling it 'the most toxic plant growing in Britain', and then suggests it has just the product for killing it off.[48] Blasting one toxic thing with another seems perverse, given that the run-off could enter a watercourse and kill all the fish, and anything that might subsequently eat them. It is over 50 years since Rachel Carson's book *Silent Spring* exposed the destruction of wildlife through the widespread use of pesticides; have we learned so little since then?[49]

As well as plants we see a long-tongued, ginger bee-fly as we walk, a furry mimic that hovers low in the canal verge, sucking nectar from the tiny blue flowers of some common speedwell with its long, needle-like proboscis.

The real bees are about too, sniffing out the early blooms. A tiny wren flits from a hedge, across the towpath and onto the deck of a moored narrowboat, where it disappears among a confusion of flower pots, and a grey wagtail hunts for early insects on the wing.

Walking with Annie, the Cut begins to seem richer than it appears at first sight in many ways – our plant list proves that there's much more to this urban canal verge than raggedy rye-grass – but our conversation makes it seem poorer. The dereliction and anonymity that allowed the towpath to be as wild as it was when Annie first experienced it isn't something to yearn for; the canal is well loved and well used now and that is a definitely a good thing. But Annie's descriptions of how it once was makes me think it could be greener than it is, and there could certainly be a lot less dog poo and dumping. Verdant verges would make this stretch of the canal between Victoria Park and the tunnel at Angel more engaging for everyone who uses it; denser greenery and growth would make it more of the linear park it claims to be.

I walk the same route again, alone, a few weeks later, missing Annie. Spring is well under way now and many more flowers are in bloom, making identification a little easier without her expert eyes to guide. I'm able to add a few more species to the list, including bladder campion, common comfrey, creeping buttercup, daisy and dog rose; herb-Robert, honeysuckle and nipplewort; ragwort, red clover and ribwort plantain. I'm gradually, plant by plant, satiating that desire to name.

8. homecoming

Humans' relationship with boats dates back to ancient times. Boats are there in the earliest poems and paintings. They have allowed us to travel, to discover, to understand, to exploit. Our history is wound up with water, and we have spent thousands of years messing about on boats. For S. and me, a boat is enabling us to create a first home together. It is also forcing us to sever ties every two weeks, to unknot our ropes, pull out our pins and move on. We have settled down in a most unsettling sort of way. But, as Jeanette Winterson suggests in reverse, in her memoir *Why Be Happy When You Could Be Normal?*, why be normal if you could be happy?

Everyone's idea of what makes a home – and what it is to feel at home – is different. What it means to me has naturally had to shift since moving onto Pike. Winterson writes that 'home is much more than shelter; home is our centre of gravity', and I tend to agree. When home is just physical shelter, it can come to feel like no home at all. But what does it mean if your home, your centre of gravity, constantly moves? What are the consequences of all this journeying about?

Most of all, it adds to my sense that we now inhabit a liminal space, that we live on the margins and are forever crossing thresholds. When we are in transit, the boat is no longer home but transportation. Machine not shelter. We stay outside when we cruise, and I think this is a distancing from our own domesticity as much as it is a practicality. The minute we moor, the boat transforms back, and we retreat inside to regroup.

In her musings about what makes a home, Winterson explores how 'nomadic people learn to take their homes with them – and the familiar objects are spread out or re-erected from place to place'. Pike makes this re-erection easy. Wherever we moor becomes ours because the boat and her contents are there. But she inevitably absorbs something of her new surroundings and so, while she is materially the same at the end of each journey, she is also different. Home can be as mercurial as the Cut.

In spite of this instability, I feel more at ease on the boat than I do anywhere else, and the feeling was almost instantaneous. In fact, moving heightens my attachment to her. When contemplating that most famous of all boaters, Odysseus, Winterson writes 'the journey is about coming home', which makes me think that while each journey

S. and I make aboard Pike is an uprooting, it is also a kind of homecoming.

It's a bright sunny day and a breeze agitates the water. Last night I dreamed that S. and I were drowning, together, holding hands. This morning I feel odd. The engine is on, warming up, and the boat is all of a buzz and a rumble. The engine room doors are fastened right back, and the top hatch pushed all the way open on its runners. I look down from the rear deck at the water, gauging the size of the surface ruffles, and then up at the treetops. Wind can be one of our greatest foes when cruising – a strong gust can catch hold of a long-sided boat, whip it round and pin it to the bank, something we have discovered first-hand, to our dismay. Today it's not too bad, just a gentle and consistent sort of blowing, nothing we can't manage. We keep the long, hinged handle for the tiller inside when it's not being used, so I pull it out and slip it on, securing it in place with a large brass pin. S. joins me on deck, smiling pale blue eyes and tar-black coffee steaming from green and brown cup. *Ready?*

Hidden behind dark glasses, I survey the slipping scene. It's classic urban idyll – formal parkland, glinting slate water and low-flying bridges, roughed up by great big bushes of buddleia, road roar, high-rises and graffiti blasts, all amplified by the sunny day and a holiday spirit. Everyone has Easter Monday off and is wild with it; this is east London and people have dressed up to hang out. The slim, slow crawling Cut is a magazine editor's dream. S. and I are part of all this, the eastern myth, our journey an act in a spring pageant.

As we slide west we pass parkland and private moorings, that offside chapel with its rude sparrow music, and then warehouses and backyards. New buildings face onto the canal but older ones turn their backs to it; the waterway hasn't always been seen as an attractive feature that can push the value of a property up. After passing under Mare Street, the canal runs parallel with a road for a while, gasometers and boats on the off side. The Cut is particularly wide here and busy with boats, moored three abreast in places. Being willing to double- or triple-moor like this is wise. It can feel like an imposition when you pull alongside another vessel and block out all its light, but it means there are far more stopping options. We tend to get to know our neighbours better when we are moored side-by-side for a few days and, in the outside position, I often feel happier one step removed from the clamour of the towpath. Getting on and off Pike is more complicated though; it's more of a climb and a clamber than a step up. The fear of falling in – or dropping something vital – is strong. The strangest thing about breasting up is when windows align and you each have a view into the other's cabin.

The pathway is as busy with people today as the Cut is with boats. Broadway Market has a powerful draw for Londoners and tourists alike. The crowds overspill onto the towpath and the area around the lock. Some boats make the most of it, opening up to sell coffee, cake and second-hand clothes.

I count 30 people lounging around on the lock gates, posing, picnicking and getting high. S. waits below with the boat while I go up alone to set things up. It feels weird to enter this space and change the dynamic from lazy to purposeful. People have to shift out of my way; the narrow eyes that track my movements around the gates are vaguely interested but also annoyed. Shy, I find operating in front of this audience traumatic, but I've found I can retreat inwards to a calm detached space if I put my mind to it. I'm here but not really here at all. I'm dropping this paddle and heaving this gate shut but inside I'm a million miles away, somewhere empty and alone, with a deafening wind that blocks everything else out. A man rises and interrupts, offering to help. I accept. He asks questions about how it all works and, funnily, I find myself enjoying explaining the physics of it, the how and the why.

Canal locks allow boats to climb hills, and Leonardo da Vinci is credited with inventing this type.[50] There are two sets of gates – top and bottom – and a chamber between them where the travelling boat can sit. Both the top and bottom lock gates have openings in them (sluices), which are blocked by paddles. A boater can open and close the sluices using a windlass (a portable crank) to raise and drop the paddles. It is by opening and closing the sluices that water is allowed in and out of the chamber, raising or lowering the water level inside, and in turn moving the boat up or down.

Another person gets up to help and suddenly we are getting through this lock a lot quicker than on a normal weekday when nobody else is around. Today we are moving uphill through the lock and, because the last person to use it was travelling in the same direction as us, I first have to empty it to get the water level inside the chamber to match the lower water level outside of it, where Pike sits and waits. I do this by pulling the top gates shut and using my windlass to drop the gate paddles and hence close the top sluices. I then wind up the paddles on the bottom gates, opening the bottom sluices to let the water rush out. It's a bit like putting a plug in at the top and pulling one out at the bottom. Once enough water has emptied out, and the level inside and outside the lock chamber is equal, I'm able to push the bottom gates open. The top gates will stay shut, the huge pressure exerted by the water on the higher level holding them securely in place. S. drives the boat in, I shut the gates behind him and drop its paddles (put the bottom plug back in). I then wind up the paddles on the top gates (pull the top plug out), again creating openings in the gates, this time to let the water rush in and fill the lock back up.

A few boats arrive as the lock is filling, heading east. They moor up and come over and it all gets quite jolly for a while. There's an older couple on a handsome red and green narrowboat. Their water tank has broken so they are heading to the Lee and then north, back to their marina so they can get it fixed. The other vessel contains a friend's ex-boyfriend, who we haven't seen in years. It's good to see him; we'd forgotten how sweet and earnest he is. His hair has grown so long. A boater who has been living on the canal for just six weeks shows up on a bike, on his way to get some water at Victoria Park. He is friendly and fresh and enquiring. We also meet a Danish family holidaying in London, who tell us they love taking canal boat trips in the UK.

As the water level inside the lock rises, so do we. Once we are level with the higher body of water, we can swing the top gates open and exit the lock. It's good etiquette to drop the paddles and close the gates behind, but if some-one's waiting to travel down it's not necessary. In all, passing through a lock takes about fifteen minutes; sometimes it's quicker, sometimes a lot slower. The average rise of a lock on the Regent's Canal is two and a half metres, and each takes 250 cubic metres of water to fill.

A.P. Herbert describes 'the precise and delicate ritual' of going through a lock in his novel *The Water Gipsies*, published in 1930. The story follows Jane Bell and the Green family travelling north from Brentford to Birmingham on the narrowboat Adventure, with Prudence the butty in tow. We hear and see 'the noisy spouts of water, the surge and gurgle under the surface, and the two boats mounting swiftly up the shining walls', and then, at length, 'the sudden quiet [as] the boats [ride] level with the lock-side'. Herbert is completely right, there is indeed 'something satisfying to the simple soul in the filling of a lock or in the rising of the tide; something complete and definite and powerful has been accomplished'. If the passage through a lock is smooth, I often hop back onto the boat aching but with a strong sense of achievement.

We journey onwards, scanning the banks for somewhere to stop. We keep to the right, searching for a Pike-sized gap or a similar-sized boat we could double-moor with. There's nothing above the lock or around the

Kingsland Basin but a suitable space materialises in Hoxton, close to the Rosemary Branch theatre pub. With some difficulty, we slot ourselves in and turn the engine off. The manoeuvre required is tricky, the water uncomfortably shallow and the canal verge hard and dry. It takes us a long time and a lot of brute force to punch in pins and securely tie Pike to the bank. The journey ends with grazed knees and rope burns. We argue, briefly, and then swallow it down and make up. There's little point rowing over troubles like these. A new home then. There's a readjustment of one's personal compass to make, maybe a couple of minutes with a map if it's somewhere we haven't moored previously, and then we're ready to continue as before. It has to be quick, we're both working tonight.

9. rites

Whenever someone gets dreamy-eyed about our drifting way of living we're careful to tell them just how challenging it can be. We are free of earthly ties but we're also free of everyday conveniences. We have to fetch our own water and deal intimately with our own waste. We have to create our own power and our own heat. We find ourselves bound to our boat in a way one never could be to bricks and mortar. Sometimes it's a joy and others it's a drain. It is always a big commitment.

The infrastructure we rely on in order to live is old and under pressure but it just about works. There are water taps at intermittent points along the towpath and special sluices where we can empty our 'black waste'. At the moment there are only two sluices and just four water points on the Regent's Canal.[51] Considering the high number of boats using this waterway, this provision is barely adequate. Three things would ease congestion and make cruising boaters' lives better: more water points, more black waste sluices and more mooring rings on concrete canal edges that mooring pins can't penetrate.

Because towpath water taps are scarce, fresh water that we can drink, cook and clean with is always an issue. Ours is stored in a 200-gallon tank at the front of Pike. When we turn on a tap or the shower, an electric pump kicks in to pull the water through the pipes. We are cautious about how much we use, and try to save and recycle it. We will catch cold water in a bucket before it runs hot and tip it into a filter jug to drink, and we brush our teeth with only the meanest of trickles. We 'borrow' water in much the same way we 'borrow' power – I often take a small, empty water bottle out with me and bring a full one back, just as I might take a dead mobile phone to the studio where I work and return with a fully charged one. We're also conscious that our grey water – the water from the sinks and the shower – ends up in the Cut. It's important we don't tip anything down the drain that will harm the aquatic environment. Things like milk, oil, bleach, non-ecological cleaning products and toiletries with micro-beads in them will all harm the flora and fauna we share the canal with.

Right now the engine room smells ripe, overripe even. Like something nasty is brewing in there. Which it is. We store our black waste from the toilet in this space at the back of the boat in what are called cassettes, small tanks that slide in and out of the toilet and have to be emptied by hand. The warm weather has arrived and the stored shit has started to stew in the heat. The cassettes are well sealed and should never leak, but smells escape. Faint ones, vegetal wisps, odorous reminders that we need to make a trip to the sluice.

It's impossible to say how long each cassette will take to fill and therefore how often they need to be emptied. Each cassette can hold seventeen litres of waste. We have a few so that, rather than empty one the moment it's full, we can store the waste for a while so anything solid can liquify. This drawn-out decomposition and its emissions are gruesome, but it makes our lives a lot easier when it comes to pouring the poo out. We add sweet-smelling, organic chemicals to the mix to aid the decomposition process.

On the Regent's Canal we have a choice between two black waste disposal sluices – known as 'Elsan points' – at St Pancras Cruising Club and Victoria Park. The facilities at the Cruising Club are nicer – there's more privacy and the sluice is better kept – but Victoria Park is closer to our current mooring in Hoxton. We decide to take a couple of cassettes there by bicycle as it will be quicker than by boat. It's hard work, physically and psychologically. It is a strange thing to cycle along a busy footpath towing a couple of containers of poo behind you. A full cassette weighs about seventeen kilograms and makes horrendous slopping sounds when you move it about.

An Elsan point is in essence an extra-large drain with a flush. Happily Victoria Park's is open air so we won't suffocate in the fetid, foul airs we are about to release. Each cassette has a spout and a pressure release valve, and there's no special equipment needed to empty one, just rubber gloves, a length of hose and a strong stomach. You unscrew the cassette, up-end it and let the waste flow down the drain. It comes out at speed and it's important to beware splashback. That said, sometimes a lot of encouragement in the form of shaking is required to get everything out. After the waste is out, the cassette needs to be rinsed thoroughly until the water runs clear. We then add cleaning fluid, shake that around, rinse again and leave the little tank to breathe.

This sluice at the park is under intense pressure from the hundreds of boats that use it, and it often becomes clogged. Fancy quilted loo roll and baby wipes don't break down, catch on the grill and form stinking lumps. The scene that presents itself can be mind-bogglingly bad at times. The sluice is in a yard just off a busy section of towpath, so this wretched job has to be performed within a metre of the passing public. I have heard many a wrinkle-nosed child ask their parents why it smells quite so offensive in this spot by Old Ford Lock. I imagine many haven't a clue of the liquid nightmares that occur just behind the gate.

Living on a boat is an exercise in letting go, in letting oneself go, in losing one's squeamishness about black waste and relaxing when it comes to having a wash. We have running water – sometimes that water is even hot – but the supply isn't infinite. Personal hygiene has thus been one of my greatest torments since moving onto Pike. I worry about running out of water so I ration my showers but I am also terrified that I smell. As a landlubber, I religiously showered every morning and then blow-dried my hair. It's not possible to do this anymore – it takes too long to heat the water in the morning, vast quantities of it are required to sustain daily showers and a steady stream of 240-volt electricity is needed to power a hairdryer. We could in theory do all these things if we were happy to burn through heinous amounts of diesel and constantly refill our water tank, but we're not.

Our limited resources have bred a conservatism with water and power that has, over time, proved surprisingly liberating. It took a few months but I am now fairly relaxed about showers. We boil water on the stove or gas for a hot wash morning and night but full showers are limited to twice a week. As I reduced the amount of time I spent washing and drying my hair, it went through a period when it looked very sad, but eventually that passed. Now my hair actually looks worst when I have just washed it.

We're only ostensibly off-grid and definitely not self-sufficient – we rely on water and fuel from the land, not to mention food – but I love the fact we are not wedded to the mains. We have achieved a degree of independence in a city setting, where it is so easy to over-consume and demand our every whim be met. On the boat we are part of 'the system', as much as we might like to think we are outside of it, but I appreciate the fact we could survive solo if we absolutely had to. I also understand my impact on the environment more clearly than ever, and I am finding further ways to reduce it.

Alan Wildman, chairman of the Residential Boat Owners' Association once said in an interview with the BBC: 'Living afloat is arguably the most sustainable, lowest impact way to live.'[52] In his essay 'Living on Infrastructure: Community and Conflict on the Canal Network', designer, writer and sometime boater David Knight takes it further, suggesting that living aboard is 'a manifest refutation of the culture of excess'. It's impossible to know the true shape of other people's private lives – and, on water as on land, using planet-friendly products and installing technology like solar panels is not compulsory. However, canal boating certainly brings all who do it into close contact with the natural world, and encourages us to respect the fact that resources are finite. We can see that the wider environment is directly affected by our actions. S. and I use significantly less water and electricity than we did in our old flat, and at least half of our self-generated power is clean and renewable.

— ◆◆◆ —

With the onset of spring, the wild ones seem more present than ever. The coots, those red-eyed buoyant brutes, are the Regent's Canal's most over-the-top aggressors and especially territorial at this time of year. The birds' piercing squeaks and shouts resound down the Cut. There's a pair here that doggedly patrol the stretch of water outside the boat, swimming back and forth, back and forth, necks bowed low to the water, tail and slate-black body feathers puffed up, white head plate skimming the water and creating a wash. The birds have taken to gathering the shredded plastic and twigs they find in the canal and stuffing both into one of our car tyre fenders. I'm not sure what we'd do if they actually decided to lay eggs; for now no one has moved in, it's more of a deposit box. Coots build the most elaborate nests. My favourite is further west at King's

Cross. Tucked beneath a concrete lip, just where York Way crosses the canal, is a coot clucking defiantly atop a shallow bowl-shaped nest of peach polystyrene (takeaway carton), blue polyethylene (plastic bag), green PET (plastic bottle) and a garden leek.

In contrast, Hoxton's moorhens are shy, although agile. They hide themselves away in the canal's offside margins but will actively explore the moored boats, climbing up ropes and picking their way around on deck when they think nobody is about. A more diminutive rail than the coot, the moorhen grows in stature when it steps out of the water. It is gawkish but smart, with its smooth brown-black feathers and white side stripe, its yellow-tipped red bill, its 'giant ooze-treading clawspread' and 'toy-grotesque' legs, as Ted Hughes so magnificently describes in his poem 'The Moorhen'. In *Birds in London*, W.H. Hudson reveals that the moorhen was almost unknown in the capital twenty years before he sat down to write in 1898, and that even then the coot, heron and cormorant were still only occasional visitors. Despite its nervous disposition, the moorhen is now, next to the mallard, Britain's most widespread water bird,[53] we see herons and cormorants most weeks, and the coot is common as muck.

The Canada goose is another of our most visible canal birds. Like the coots, the geese patrol the Cut territorially, fog-horning about their water rights. Most have lost their migratory instincts, remaining here all year round, feeding on grass and some aquatic plants, as well as hunks of tossed bread. At the moment, three pairs of geese wrangle outside the boat on a daily basis; two pairs have young, one pair has none. The geese with young seem to move about together happily enough but the ones without cause a commotion every time they all chance to meet. The adults bob and snake their necks wildly, honking all the time, and at least two of the birds will draw themselves up, drumming their wings against the water and pushing out great waves that in turn slap against the moored boats and make the goslings reel about. These antics always attract a crowd.

The geese are some of the largest birds on the Cut but the mute swans are bigger and sit at the top of the canal's avian hierarchy. Yesterday, at dusk, two Canada geese and their three small goslings were resting on some shallow stone steps that lead out of the canal opposite the Rosemary Branch pub. I'm projecting, but they seemed sleepy and content. A pair of swans with four cygnets arrived from the west, gliding in all regal and serene, two of the young tucked up on the female's back. Thirty seconds of hissing chaos ensued and the goslings were unceremoniously evicted. Suddenly it was the cygnets installed on the steps, and the goose family was retreating into the distance.

I watch all this from a perch on Pike's roof. Now the weather is decent, I'm building a small garden up here. It has to be kept fairly free for practical things like fuel, life-buoys, barge poles and ropes, but a decent amount of space can be given over to gardening. The plants are growing in a three-metre-by-one-metre open wooden box positioned towards the bow. The box is secured to the boat but slightly raised off the steel to stop water puddling underneath, which would cause the paint to blister. It's split into three one-metre-square compartments. I'm focusing on herbs, bee- and butterfly-friendly flowers and edible leaves. I'm feeling ambitious but there are a few constraints. It's important the rooftop plants don't overly obscure sight lines from the stern and so make cruising difficult. The plants also have to fit under low bridges and be compact enough to withstand high winds.

The boat top is slowly coming to life with sprouts, shoots and clusters of blooms. Calendula, hyssop and nasturtium seeds have become healthy, thrusting young plants. Love-in-the-mist is following on behind with its first few filigree fronds. I've sown salad leaves like chervil and rocket in an old fruit box I found on the street. Geranium has bunches of scarlet flowers and French lavender is in full purple and white bloom. Sedum cloud walker is set to burst into dirty pink flower at any moment and calamintha is secreting a sweet peppermint scent. The sage and garden mint look less healthy. I expect they have an entirely understandable aversion to drinking canal water, which I scoop directly out of the Cut with my metal can.

It is while we are in Hoxton, enjoying the plants, the waterfowl and the spring weather, that we become concerned about Pike, who has developed a pronounced list on her port side. We toy with the subject for a few days, debating whether she has always leaned a little to the left. Why is it more noticeable now? Is it because we are spending more time outside and so looking more closely? The canal is shallow here, could we have beached? None of the other boats seem to have run aground. We don't have an especially low draught; there's no reason why we would beach when nobody else has, unless we have hit some kind of shelf. Desperate, we wonder if it is because all the heavy things we have – the washing machine, the shower, the oven, the kitchen sink, most of our music and books – are on that side of the boat. We can definitely agree that our boat is listing, and that it appears to be getting worse, but we don't know why or what to do about it.

Later I decide to check below the inspection hatches, something we neglectfully haven't done all winter. It never seems like a pressing job. And I don't, even at this point, connect checking under the hatches with the list. It just comes into my head as a job to do and so I do it. It involves pulling out the back step that leads from the engine room into the living cabin, and then lifting a small flap, which allows a view into the cabin bilge and a section of the hull. There's another inspection hatch by the washing machine. The idea is to use these port and starboard hatches to check the hull every so often to make sure it is dry, that no water is leaking in or out.

A bit of boat anatomy is probably needed here: the hollow area below the floorboards (and technically under-water) is called the cabin bilge. This space is filled with ballast, in our case broken concrete flagstones, which balance the boat, giving it weight and stability in the water. It should be dry. The hull is coated with bitumen on the outside to prevent rust but on the inside it's bare, unprotected steel.

I lift the inspection hatch and instead of a small section of hull, I see my own face darkly reflecting back up at me. This is when the rushing in my ears starts and my chest begins its hollowing out. I lift the second inspection hatch and again see myself. The cabin bilge is not just a little damp or a bit puddly; the water is about a foot deep. I break the news to S. in a blur. The most important thing now is to bail the water out. The hatches cover only small openings into the bilge and so the bailing has to be done with a plastic pint glass, awkwardly scooped in and poured out into a bucket. The water is clear and it doesn't smell – we use these facts to reassure ourselves that it could just as easily be water from the tank as water from the canal. Far, far better to have an internal leak than a crack in the hull. We empty the water from inside the hatches and it immediately refills, right to the top. This is the moment that our hearts drop. Pike is listing because her cabin bilge is completely full of water, the concrete ballast sodden like a sponge, and if we don't get it emptied out we could sink. Where on earth is the water coming from? If she does have a crack in her hull we are in big trouble.

We empty the bilge over the next few hours, crouched in our corners, on our knees, scooping the water out, emptying glass after glass into bucket after bucket. We remove hundreds of gallons of water this way. The repetitive bailing means we don't have to think about anything else, we don't have to speak. It takes hours to reach the point where the water is too shallow to bail and we can start using towels. It's then a laborious process of wringing out. Once we reach the soaking-it-up-with-newspaper stage, we have to start addressing the fact we have a major leak but no idea where the water is coming from, what it means or what can be done. It's a lonely feeling. Our precious home, our dear Pike, is soaked and threatening to sink.

We trawl online forums to find out how other people have dealt with such incidents, and write a long checklist of the things that could have caused the flood. The last thing on the list is a crack in the hull. Please anything but that. There are a lot of other things it could be. Despite the despair and exhaustion, we are in a much better position than we have been for weeks. The list has dramatically reduced now the build-up of water is out. But we have the terrible knowledge that something serious is wrong. No more ignorant bliss.

Working out where the water is coming from ends up taking a few days and a lot of sleuthing. In the meantime, we continue to bail the water, which no longer fills the bilge beneath the inspection hatches right to the top but gradually seeps out from the wet flagstones to be soaked up with tea towels and newspaper. We are getting low on water we can use to drink, wash and cook but are loath to fill up our tank until we discover and fix the leak. So we start bringing water back home in five-litre bottles, filled up at my studio, stuffed into rucksacks and panniers, and cycled across town. We find other places to shower.

We pull everything out of the kitchen cupboards and wrap kitchen towel around all of the pipes to see if the paper gets wet overnight. We pull up floorboards in the living room, bedroom and bathroom. We eventually discover a small puddle behind some panelling at the bottom of a bathroom cabinet. The source of the water is an unbelievably tiny, slow drip; a loose connection between two pipes. It must have taken months, almost a year even, for this pathetic dribble to fill the cabin bilge up. We buy a new T-connector and fit it ourselves. The entire job costs £7.68.

Although we do sometimes wonder what on earth we're doing, getting to grips with our vessel's quirks means we have started to understand how our home works in more detail than we ever would have bothered to in a flat. The fact that it is so hard to find someone to help out – marine mechanics, specialist electricians and plumbers aren't easy to find in town – means you have to do it yourself. It will take months for Pike's bilge to dry out – and a few weeks for us to get over this excitement – but now the leak is fixed, fear has been replaced with a certain amount of satisfaction. We had a major incident to contend with and we sorted it out ourselves. It is empowering to solve our own problems like this, to master new mind-benders like dramatic lists. Pike pays back our efforts with gratifying directness. We get what we give.

10. fragments

Inside the boat I sit and listen. The sun bounces off a tower block's windows and beams bright into the living room, making me squint. Squealing kids on kayaks crash into our side, thwacking Pike with their paddles as they try to push off. Behind me, loose piano-key paving slabs dip and rise. For cyclists unfamiliar with the terrain, the sudden fluidity of the towpath here is disconcerting and the concrete's discordant ripple is quickly followed by the squeal of brakes.

The slabs are loose for a reason. A 400-kilovolt cable runs under the path, stretching for six miles from Lisson Grove to the mouth of the Hertford Union, and the flagstones are unfixed for access. It was cheaper for the electricity company to buy the towpath than to dig up major roads to lay the cable, and the canal water can be used to keep the wires cool.[54]

Running shoes pound the path, distant, close, distant. There's fast-stepping heel on stone, heel on stone, heel on stone. Someone in a hurry, smartly dressed. Walk, jog, brake. Tap, slap, screech. The sounds roll around inside our echo box of a boat. There's a heavy hum of bridge traffic, mixed up with sirens and birdsong. Words filter in too, the dislocated bones of conversations. An angry voice bubbles up, spurts and spills out of a neighbouring boat. A painful break-up. Despair laid bare on voyeurs' creek.

On the Cut, home is as public as it is private, and as political as it is personal. As the numbers attest, boating is contagious. What was once eccentric and rare is increasingly common. The Canal and River Trust – the organisation that currently manages the UK's inland waterways, after British Waterways was privatised in 2012 – reports a significant rise in boat numbers on the London network between 2007 and March 2014, from 2,175 to 2,964 boats. These figures include boats on residential moorings as well as vessels that are continuously cruising.[55] In 2011 there were 626 boats sited at casual and visitor moorings across London's waterways, and this number increased to 957 in 2013, a figure that includes visitors as well as people who call this city home.[56] In 2014, the Canal and River Trust report that overall boat numbers rose by 14 per cent, while the number of continuous cruisers in east London apparently increased by 85 per cent.[57] The network is large – London has approximately 100 miles of canal corridor, covering

270 hectares[58] – but cruising boats understandably tend to concentrate in the rare areas where there are essential water and waste facilities.

If there are almost 3,000 boats like ours in London, both moored and cruising about, they could easily be providing homes for 4,000 people, assuming some are home to more than one person. Potentially more, depending on how many live on each craft. It sounds like a lot – and it is – but it is worth noting that back in the 1870s more than 40,000 people lived on boats on the UK's canals; today it is estimated to be around 11,000.[59]

The fact it's getting busier makes life on the water more complex – it's more of an effort to find spaces to moor when you are competing with hundreds of other boats, and the pressure on water and waste disposal points increases. There's a lot to love about continuous cruising and being able to call more than one part of London home, but our life is not one of idle roving, following the city winds wherever they take us. The Cut is far from bucolic, and itinerancy comes with stigma attached. Since moving onto Pike we have found ourselves justifying our existence a lot. Friends, family and strangers alike interrogate our domestic set-up much more than they would if we were living in a house. The public nature of our peripatetic lives, coupled with our decision not to do the usual thing, fascinates some people and makes others nervous, perhaps believing our unconventional choices to be a judgement on their own conventional ones. Without brick walls, we become alien. A friend of ours who works in local government recently told us that, as boaters, we are now classed as 'hard to reach'.

The most shocking discovery since moving onto the water is that, despite the fact I have now actually bought my own home, without a residential postal address I am technically classed as homeless. If I want to be eligible to vote in the upcoming election I will have to register as such.[60] I feel like I am being forced to opt out, that I am being made hard to reach. Without a fixed abode, a lot of other things become complicated too, including banking and healthcare. I use my work studio address for most things, but that's not possible when registering to vote. To be honest, I fear for my credit rating. I can't help it, it's clearly been hard-wired. It's difficult to shake off such mind-forged manacles even if you have escaped some of the physical ones. I don't actually want to exist outside of society; I want to live on a boat and still feel like I belong. I want to live on a boat and be able to vote without registering as homeless, because I'm not.

Canal boating doesn't tend to get that much attention from the national press, except the occasional property story – *Couple survive in extraordinarily small space! Buy your student daughter a boat instead of a flat!* However, there was an interesting article focusing specifically on London boaters in the *Guardian* in 2014. It was realistic, featuring several interviews with continuous cruisers, the head of the Canal and River Trust, a local Labour councillor and some residents who live close to the canal in King's Cross. Everyone quoted seemed reasonable and what they said fair enough, except for the councillor, who suggested it was unacceptable that people living on boats should want to send their children to school in Islington or vote in an election in the borough. He flagged up the fact boaters use public services but don't pay council tax.[61]

Other than education, the councillor doesn't elaborate about what public services boaters are supposedly exploiting, but the council tax argument doesn't provide a clear justification for excluding boaters in the way he might like. National income tax, not local council taxes, pays for education, and everyone is entitled to vote. We may only live in places part-time, but we are still affected by local issues and decision making. It's not unreasonable for us to want to be able to have a say.

The councillor's comments have bruised the atmosphere for me, and planted the idea firmly in my head that some people see us as pariahs. I worry when I go to empty the food waste we've collected. I don't pay council tax here in Hoxton and so technically I have no right to recycle, but what other option is there? I am braced to be challenged, rehearsing in my head what I'll say if I am. Rather than a drain on resources, I would argue boaters are actually good neighbours to have. We help keep areas alive, not just aesthetically by injecting some idiosyncrasy into the cityscape, but by using local businesses and providing towpath safety of sorts.

Any long-term Londoner will testify that the towpath, especially in east London, has gone from downright dangerous in places to vibrant and, generally, safer feeling, especially at night. There's still crime but cyclists and boaters have both bravely reclaimed the space and, in turn, given more pedestrians the confidence to follow. People's routes are now flanked by protective vessels, with the likelihood of a helping hand on board should one be needed. From our boat we've provided travel advice, puncture repair and even a cup of tea for an unfortunate who fell in. It works both ways, and we often find ourselves relying on the kindness of strangers. When the mooring ropes of our boat and those of two of our neighbours were untied by a group of bored kids, three passers-by on the towpath did all they could to help us grab the lines and stop the boats drifting off. A man even jumped aboard one of the loose vessels as it careered out into the waterway and was nearly washed away himself. The sense of community, of neighbourliness, between boater and towpath-user was strong.

'If there's one thing that revolutionary communists and bankers can agree on, it is that there is a housing crisis in Britain', writes Rowan Moore in the *Observer*.[62] In 2014, fewer than 142,000 new homes were built; the recommended amount was 240,000.[63] London is at the epicentre of the crisis, which Moore describes as 'an accelerating human disaster', one that is creating 'exploitative landlords, overcrowding and low-quality homes'. In the capital, it's also pushing people further and further out. In fact, in the past two years, 2,707 council tenant families have been moved from their homes in London to places as far afield as Bradford, Pembrokeshire and Plymouth.[64] It's absurd for local politicians to suggest their neighbourhoods no longer have room for people earning low to average incomes, and that if such people can't afford sky-rocketing house prices or rents they should simply leave.[65] Rowan Moore underlines the consequences:

It's hard to run a business if your employees find it hard to get a home. If people on low and middle incomes are pushed out, big cities will in course lose those who make, maintain and repair things, who care for the ill and old, who clean, who cook and wait in restaurants, and who look after and teach children. The creative and inventive types, currently such a big part of London's sales pitch to the world, will go too.

In this context it makes sense for London's waterways to provide a place for some people to live, as they always have done. There's not room for lots of people to decamp to the canal – and let's be honest, most wouldn't want to give up 240-volt electricity, a flushing toilet, central heating and a postal address – but in the midst of a housing crisis, as London continues her endless evolution, we cannot be protectionist about the Cut or its proper use. The point and purpose of man-made waterways is as unfixed as boaters are.

David Knight's essay 'Living on Infrastructure: Community and Conflict on the Canal Network' is a brief study of what it means to live permanently on the UK's inland waterways, something he believes challenges all our assumptions about what good housing and good communities are. Knight suggests that living a low-impact life on infrastructural waters could be seen as 'a lived statement in counterpoint to bankrupted ideas of property as investment', and that continuous cruisers are 'abandoning the idea of land ownership' and so achieving 'a strong sense of autonomy and freedom'. Changes in the way the waterways are managed threaten this, and he warns that a 'spirit of heritage' could 'calcify a viable and rewarding existence whilst failing to learn from it'. Instead of alienating those who take to the water, maybe we should pause to ask boat dwellers what they can teach us.

When people declare London's canals are congested or even full up, and talk about live-aboard boaters as if we're a problem that needs to be solved, it's hard not to panic. The rules governing cruising boats' movements are a grey area, and the infrastructure creaks, but generally the system works. Importantly, it is completely legal for those of us without a residential mooring to make use of London's canals and rivers. As the current Chief Executive of the Canal and River Trust had to publicly state, 'The right for boaters to continuously cruise is enshrined in law'.[66]

The 1995 British Waterways Act clearly says licensed travelling boats must move every fourteen days but it does not specify how far the boat must travel or define what an acceptable cruising pattern is.[67] The Act does not require boats to be on a progressive journey, merely that boats be used 'bona fide for navigation'.[68] Despite this right to a fortnight, stay times at popular visitor moorings are being reduced. In east London, sections of the Regent's Canal at Broadway Market and Victoria Park now only allow boats to moor for a week at a time. The Canal and River Trust has also said it plans to refuse to renew the licenses of cruising boats that it doesn't consider to be moving far enough, unless the boater finds a permanent mooring.[69]

The Trust is trying to manage a busy UK network, and working harder than before to enforce the two-week rule and keep vessels moving, but it simply does not have the legal authority to define what a reasonable distance over a year is. How far is far enough is contentious, and so the licensing situation for boaters without a home mooring starts to feel worryingly vague. Losing your license would be disastrous. Since long-term moorings in London are rare, you would effectively be made homeless, for real this time, not just on paper for the purposes of getting a vote. Should such a mooring become available in town, the Canal and River Trust's controversial auction process could push the rent to over £20,000 per year.[70] More reasonably priced community and private moorings are uncommon. High mooring fees mean a less diverse boating community, and in turn a London with diminished personality.

Privatisation of once-public moorings is another very real threat. We have learned that our beloved stretch of bank at Leyton Marsh is no longer free for cruisers to moor alongside. Our recent stay there has been recast as a last hurrah. The change was swift and sudden. The boats that happened to be moored there one fortuitous day received letters from the Lee Valley Regional Park Authority inviting them to become paying tenants. Apparently only good-looking boats were asked to stay. For many the process felt stealthy, underhand. Once open to all but now only to a rent-paying few, it bodes ill for the future. The boats that can now moor there permanently aren't getting much for their money – there's no running water, mains electricity or waste disposal on site, which tenants might reasonably expect – but they do get the convenience and security of a slice of river to call their own. The change of use means its unkempt, swampish days are likely numbered; plans for a proper path are already being discussed. Talking to some of the new tenants, it's hard to begrudge them their good fortune. They are well aware that they won a closed lottery when they were invited to stay on as residents, and they're grateful for the chance to tie on to fixed pins. The travelling life is tough and to be able to stay in one place, for them, is a relief.

But the loss of the Leyton Marsh mooring makes the position of cruising boaters feel precarious. It could well be a worrying sign of things to come, as creating private moorings out of public ones becomes a more lucrative prospect. London definitely needs more fairly priced residential moorings, where boaters can pay to stay long-term – in the same way she desperately needs homes ordinary people can afford – but they shouldn't come at the cost of existing open-to-all sites. New residential moorings could instead be created on offside banks and outside blocks of flats where it currently isn't possible to casually moor.

The Cut's bohemian days may well be numbered. Competing forces have competing visions for it, and the people who spend the most time in this landscape have little say. The argument for eccentricity isn't being heard over the noise of the diggers. Currently a haven for people finding creative ways to live in an often hostile city, there's a fear that London's waterways will gradually be closed off to cruisers, not least because, as David Knight says, 'the alternative way of life represented by living aboard does not always sit neatly with the watercolours and computer-generated imagery of the leisure and regeneration sectors'.

The early boaters were pioneers, preparing the ground for an invasion by making the waterways first fashionable, then accessible. A recent proliferation of developments boasting canal or river views – some with names redolent of Venice – shows just how desirable certain stretches have become to land dwellers as well as boaters. Old council housing blocks are being demolished to make way for luxury flats. On a towpath walk or ride you might witness such a ruin crumbling away behind high hoardings, its freshly exposed inner bricks awaiting the final blows, wallpaper to the wind.

I fear for the future shape of London, not just for her waterways. I'm not worried about ad hoc gentrification, which can often bring a breath of new life, one independent café at a time. I'm worried about the masterplanned, corporate-led squeeze that is retouching our city into something generic, smoothing out her rough edges, erasing her interesting bits. It isn't limited to the Olympic site at Stratford, it extends north, south, east and west. In his author's note to the 2010 edition of *The Unofficial Countryside*, Richard Mabey's strongest lament is not about pollution or pesticides but that 'an anaemic tidiness creeps across all the last fragments of free land'. As we witness the corporatisation and cleansing of our city, it is the canal and riverscapes with their boats and bustle and weeds and wrecks that should be left free to offer some respite.

summer

— ◆ —

heartland

Regent's Canal
Angel to Little Venice

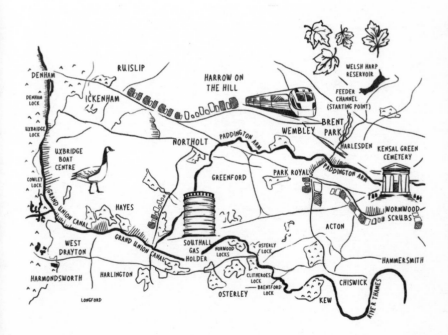

11. lost ways

We have been sucked in and swallowed up by the dark arch that drips. Its mucous, glistening walls curve in close, as though the bricks were the skin of a long, straight throat. Thin, grey stalactites grow downwards, sharp signs of a slow-motion melt. The boat noses towards a far-off speck of daylight, cleaving a dark, short-lived trail through tightly packed green weed that zips itself back up once we pass. Pike's headlamp uncovers sprayed-on tags and hieroglyphs on the inner arch, and throws bending shadows up the walls – me made gigantic and ghoulish, hooded as I am against the tunnel's dank weather and holding a ten-foot boat pole.

There is a hill between Angel and King's Cross that lies in the canal's chosen path. Instead of climbing up and over it via several locks, the waterway cuts straight through. The towpath ends abruptly in a tall brick wall and the canal disappears into darkness, folded in to its smallest possible proportions. For fifteen minutes or so we're packed in a space between the above-ground and the underground, the weight of Islington pressing down, the tube network opening up below.

The tunnel is a moody cave that changes from one journey to the next. It is full of slippery echoes, and smells of wet clay, diesel and damp. The water itself is placid, raked only by slow boats and not by the wind, but it changes colour to suit the season. In summer it draws in luminescent duckweed blooms, in winter it will darken to a colour deeper than black.

Sometimes before going in we sit at the entrance, tracking the headlight of another boat slowly sliding towards us. There's not enough room for two boats to pass. Once that boat is safely out we can enter Angel's orifice, another two or three boats perhaps following behind, single file. On those days the tunnel is full of voices and extra loud with engines. But I like it most when we have it all to ourselves. It is a safe place, an embrace, somewhere a problem can be solved or at least left well behind. Distance and time become loose things in here. It feels like it could be a portal, like we might arrive at the other end to find everything has altered or a hundred years have passed. It can also be frightening. What would happen if all this collapsed, if the weight of all those buildings and buses above got too much for the bricks to bear?

When we reach the opposite tunnel mouth, it is a

perfect 'O', the view above water reflected to create the illusion there is, in fact, no water at all and that we are travelling suspended in a perfectly round, silvered brick tube. As we slowly slip out, first the bow then the aft, cool night is replaced again with warm day.

It is in the Islington Tunnel that the connection to the past seems most strong. Even though it was renovated in 2000 – and what happens above and below it has changed beyond all recognition – the inside of the tunnel must be much as it always has been since it opened in 1820. In the early days, barge folk would leg their way through, lying on their backs and pushing their boats along by walking their feet for three-quarters of a mile across the brickwork. Their horses were guided up the hill above ground to meet the barge at the tunnel opening on the other side. Later mechanised tugs replaced leg power and pulled boats through in clouds of steam, then sulphurous smoke.

Like all London's waterways, the Cut offers us what Peter Ackroyd calls 'liquid history',[71] which I take to mean a dynamic story that continues to accumulate; a story that isn't tied to a single moment in time. The Regent's Canal collects around and within it a multitude of buildings, objects, people, memories and ideas. It courses, revolutionary, through the 19th century; it plods, depressed, through the 20th; and it emerges triumphant in the 21st. It time travels. It merges the present with the past. It has the status of heritage site, but it is not something viewed at set times and with a ticket; it's not cosseted behind ropes and glass. Old as it is, the canal still functions. The locks work, the tunnel lets us travel under Islington, the rituals and customs of canal boating stretch out across 200 years and will surely stretch on for 200 more.

The UK's thousands of miles of canal were originally built to link up already navigable waterways. Before the advent of trains and motor vehicles, the narrow, hand-dug channels made it newly possible to transport large quantities of goods into areas untouched by natural rivers. Arterial canals connect two river basins or valleys; lateral canals – like the Lee Navigation – run parallel to rivers and follow the same valley.[72]

The Grand Junction Canal – now known as the Grand Union – was built at the height of canal mania between 1793 and 1805, linking London with Birmingham. The Regent's Canal came later, opening to traffic in 1820 and connecting the canal system to the Thames Docks and, in turn, the wider world. As architectural photographer Eric de Maré declares in his book *The Canals of England*, 'this was the great canal era which made the Industrial Revolution possible'. David Knight describes how canals 'shifted the scale of the economy from the county to the nation'. Canals were a catalyst for further industrialisation and connectedness. As such, they helped change Britain's identity. Peering down at the waters of the Regent's today, I struggle to believe that something so docile could redefine our sense of nationhood, but the Industrial Revolution altered everything and set us on our future course. Canals were crucial to that.

Moving goods by way of water is extremely efficient; low friction means a lone horse can pull 80 tonnes of cargo, where it could only move two tonnes by road or ten by rail.[73] And, where oceans and rivers are unpredictable and subject to forces beyond our control, a canal is tame. As James Brindley, the master engineer behind 365 miles of the country's canals, said: 'If you lay the giant flat on his back, he loses all his force and becomes completely passive, whatever his size may be.'[74]

The people behind canal mania were in no way the first to discover how to slay the water giant, but they were the first to begin cutting artificial waterways into the UK on such a grand scale. The canal makers were pioneers and profiteers. Their epic projects helped herald in a new world order, one entirely recognisable to us: an order shaped by fossil fuel-dependent, market-driven, global mass production. By 1850, 4,000 miles of canal laced across the UK and boats using the waterways collectively carried over 30 million tonnes of freight each year.[75] The bargees who operated the boats lived on their vessels full-time, either self-employed on boats they owned – so called 'Number Ones' – or working for large transportation companies like Pickfords or Fellows, Morton & Clayton.

When London's canal system was first cut into the earth, 90 per cent of the waterways sat beyond the city's boundaries, passing prettily through rolling countryside. In *The Regent's Canal*, David Fathers describes engravings from the 1820s that show the canal surrounded by farms and woods. But London was expanding rapidly and the city soon rose to meet the water, changing its character irrevocably. All kinds of goods were carried into town by canal boat: chemicals, timber, coal, coke, ice, beer. Hay, straw and corn were barged in to feed London's horses, and manure was barged back out to fertilise the fields. Canals fed industry and encouraged further growth. In turn, wharves, warehouses, factories, power stations and gasworks were built along the Regent's east–west route.[76]

Such engravings as Fathers describes, along with watercolours and black and white photographs, can be found within the Museum of London's online archive and on display in the London Canal Museum, which is home to a small but interesting exhibition explaining the history and mechanics of the inland waterways. The Canal Museum plays a silent film following a coal barge journeying from Limehouse to Paddington in 1924 – *Barging through London* – on a loop; while British Pathé has recently made its entire film archive available online, including shorts like *The Barge Fellows – Studies on the Regent's Canal* (1926), *Regent's Canal* (1938), *Corn by Canal* (1940) and *Venice in London* (1963), all narrated in rip-roaring received pronunciation. The images, moving and still, describe something at once familiar and far away – from barely recognisable rural scenes in the earliest days to horse-drawn barges gliding through London in the 1920s, and from diesel-powered boats stoically contributing to the war effort in the forties to a glimpse of what's to come in the sixties, when that glamorous age of leisure was newly dawning. Much of the imagery paints a picture more positive than surely could have been the case.

I actively seek out the other side of the story because I know a city canal always has the potential to be foul as well as fair. The Regent's Canal opened at a time when Thomas De Quincey could indeed stand in the 'great Mediterranean of Oxford Street' and gaze, stoned, up Marylebone's avenues onto moonlit fields and woods. But this was also 19th-century London: cruel, filthy and growing apace. Oxford Street was a road that 'drinkest the tears of orphans' after all.[77] There is no doubt that the increasingly urban canals were as grim and gruesome in places as they were bucolic in others. How could a network so entwined with industry be anything else?

One of the most lurid canal-related objects in the Museum of London collection is a broadside from 1833 recounting the terrible murder of a young boy whose body was dumped in the Regent's Canal. The newspaper headline reports, verbosely, that it has 'The Full Account of a most Cruel and Diabolical Murder, Committed upon the body of Robert Pavior, a Boy aged 13. The most Revolting Deed ever laid before the Public.'[78]

Violent crime wasn't the only issue: high passions and pollution were problems too. In his essay 'Wapping Workhouse', taken from *Selected Journalism 1850–70*, Charles Dickens describes 'Mr Baker's terrible trap' – a grim canal lock that is 'baited with a scum that was like the soapy rinsing of sooty chimneys' and has become a hotspot for suicide attempts. The desperate women that run, jump and splash into the black water in the middle of the night are mostly fished out and carted off to the workhouse. Dickens learns all this from a slimy apparition who 'may have been the youngest son of his filthy old father, Thames'. The sallow man leers and gurgles as he works the lock gates, then vanishes.

Another object in the Museum of London archive – an illustration from a book called *Journeys Through London, or, Byways of Modern Babylon* by James Greenwood (undated, c. 1873) – shows Mr Dodd's dust yard, a dump that opened straight out onto the Regent's Canal. Greenwood describes a filthy scene: 'Flanking one side of the yard were a score or so of upreared dustcarts, and on the other side, extending almost from the outer gate to the water's brink, were great mounds of ordinary dustbin muck.' He goes on to describe the people who populate such a place: 'In the midst of the mounds – literally, so that in many cases part only of their bodies were visible – were thirty or forty women and girls.' Each woman possesses a large iron sieve and sifts through Londoners' discarded cinders and ash, separating the spoil into soil suitable for cultivation or making bricks. The women wear 'coarse, fingerless gloves', matched with 'great lace-up boots, such as carmen wear, and great sackcloth aprons, such as few carmen would care to be burdened with'. The archive provides more information about the dust yard owner in the form of an 1846 Post Office directory entry, which lists him as 'Dodd, Henry, scavenger, carter & road contractor, City Wharf, Eagle Wharf Road, New North Road, Hoxton'.[79]

It's possible to learn even more about canal-side dust heaps in an edition of *Household Words* from July 1850, in which Richard Henry Horne penned an intricate article called 'Dust; Or Ugliness Redeemed', reportage that helped shape Dickens' *Our Mutual Friend.* In it we meet a gaggle of 'Searchers and Sifters', including 83-year-old Peg Dotting whose wretched nose is as blue as her ragged petticoats and who hobbles along carrying a rusty iron sieve. We learn that, while the huge, dusky black mountain on the water's edge may be disgusting, it is full of human, avian and mammalian life, all just about surviving on the city's scraps.[80]

Filth and hardship were not unique to the Victorian age, and conditions on and around navigations continued to be tough well into the 20th century. George Orwell's account of the canals up north in *The Road to Wigan Pier* – published in 1937 – describes something apocalyptic. Parts of London couldn't have been any better. He underlines how harsh a winter working the waterways must have been, reporting canal paths that are 'a mixture of cinders and frozen mud, criss-crossed by the imprints of innumerable clogs', bargemen 'muffled to the eyes in sacks' and lock gates wearing 'beards of ice'. For Orwell, the canal and its environs 'seemed a world from which vegetation had been banished; nothing existed except smoke, shale, ice, mud, ashes, and foul water.'

Despite crime, pollution and harsh working conditions, the canal network was used for transporting freight for

over 150 years, although it increasingly faced fierce competition from railways and roads. Barge travel is slow and
mass production is, ultimately, all about speed. By the
1960s, not yet two decades after nationalisation in 1948,
commercial barge traffic had almost entirely ceased. The
canals had been in decline for years, but it was a deep freeze
in the winter of 1962–3 that dealt the fatal blow. The desperately cold weather made navigation, and earning a
living, impossible for months.[81] The network had already
shrunk from 4,000 miles to 2,775 miles by this point, with
abandoned canals either slowly silting up or purposely
infilled.[82] By the end of the 1960s the network's reinven-
tion from industrial to recreational landscape had begun.
Canals gradually started to open up to the public as places
to walk, cycle and go boating along, thanks in great part
to the efforts of the Inland Waterways Association and its
band of vocal volunteers.[83] The process was slow, and it
is only relatively recently that towpath walks and canal
views have become quite so popular.

In the 1990s British Waterways – the government body
then charged with maintaining the UK's canals – restyled
itself as a 'major player in the regeneration of run down
areas near waterways'.[84] Now operating as the Canal and
River Trust, this more commercial approach continues.
Canals' primary function may have changed completely

– in fact, the network no longer has a clearly defined, single purpose – but the waterways have left their mark on the UK landscape. In London, the canal has become an important source of local colour for any borough lucky enough to have been cut.

— ◆◆◆ —

We exit the Islington Tunnel and cross the border into the borough of Camden, finding a place to moor between St Pancras and King's Cross. The canal's utilitarian good looks are here in spades, and are something the area's modern-day developers have been keen to exploit. Battlebridge Basin was built in 1822 and was once home to a timber yard, a steam flour mill, corn and salt warehouses, a jam factory, a beer bottling operation and an engineering works; today, most of the buildings have been converted into offices. An old ice house is now the London Canal Museum, and the basin itself is a private residential marina. One of the office buildings has a set of decoratively defunct wall cranes, which once unloaded barrels of Guinness brought into town from Dublin via the docks.

The Imperial Gas, Light and Coke Company constructed two large gasworks on the Regent's Canal, one here and one in Haggerston. The famous King's Cross gas holders were built between 1860 and 1867 to store gas manufactured on site from coal.[85] These gasometers have recently been dismantled and reassembled in a new spot. Once complete, they will have a new, purely aesthetic purpose, encircling 145 flats and a park. This kind of preservation has happened before, when the Channel Tunnel Rail Link was being built. Rather than being demolished, the 1872 St Pancras Waterpoint – a relic from the age of steam – was moved and reassembled piece by piece in its current spot overlooking the St Pancras Cruising Club. History is particularly liquid in this area, it seems; old buildings and industrial landmarks are renovated, reimagined, even repositioned.

It is in King's Cross that I dream of the River Fleet, which is buried here beneath the Cut. If she hadn't been lost, we would be able to cruise from St Pancras along the route of Farringdon Road, past Smithfield Market, to meet the Thames at Blackfriars. The Fleet was a natural river that was used as an open sewer until the lower part was cleaned up and canalised by Christopher Wren after the Great Fire of 1666. As Peter Ackroyd explains in *London Under*, Wren 'widened the Fleet and gave it some of the characteristics of a Venetian canal, with wharves of stone on either side and with a grand new Holborn bridge'. Had it survived like this, it would be a majestic boating route. Sadly, within a few years it was again full of blood and gore from the meat market, along with many other rank and rotten things. No wonder Londoners wanted rid of this rancid ditch of disease and vice. It had been made so foul by things dumped, tipped and poured into it that its future could only lie underground. By the time the 1820s rolled in – the decade the Regent's Canal opened – the River Fleet had been all but hidden and its fate as a sewer forever sealed, remaining one to this day. It wasn't forgotten though; the gathering gases of putrefaction caused it to explode in 1846. The buried waterway is full of paraphernalia from pre-Roman times on. Everything from bones and bodies to toys, buckles and pipes have been found in its banks during excavations.

Walking the Fleet's route today – guided by Paul Talling's *London's Lost Rivers* – it is easy to mentally replace the roads with a river because they sit in an obvious valley. Holborn Viaduct never passed over the water – the Fleet was buried before it was built – but its presence underlines the area's naturally sloping banks. Street and place names provide most of the clues to the river's route. Clerkenwell and Bridewell reveal that the 'river of wells' once passed this way; there's also St Chad's Place – St Chad was the patron saint of wells – and Holborn, which stems from 'hollow stream' and refers to the Fleet's deep valley. Old Seacoal Lane and Newcastle Close hint at an era when

Farringdon Road was a navigable route north for working barges carrying fuel. Beyond geography and road names, there are two more potent pieces of evidence. It's possible to hear the Fleet rushing below a grate in the middle of Ray Street, opposite the Coach and Horses pub. It's a lively gush that tells the listener this river-cum-sewer hasn't lost all of its vigour. Further along, there is a glazed blue plaque reading 'Clerks' Well, Metropolitan Borough of Finsbury' and, close by, the preserved well itself can be viewed through a plate of glass. The outlet of the Fleet into the Thames, just west of Blackfriars Bridge, is an inconspicuous arch cut into the embankment. It's likely only noticed when purposely pointed out.

Heading downhill from King's Cross Bridge to Blackfriars, it's impossible not to think Farringdon Road would be far nicer as a navigation, with a towpath route to and from the Thames and space for cruisers to moor. The loss of the Fleet is the starkest example there is of London's capacity to mistreat her waterways. While the situation has undoubtedly improved since Wren's canalisation experiments, vast amounts of waste still regularly flood into the Thames and her tributaries. According to Thames Water, London's sewers overflow on a weekly basis, flushing 39 million tonnes of raw sewage straight into the River each year.[86] Sustainable urban drainage systems, more green spaces and fewer grey ones would go a long way to preventing this but neither seem to be a priority for the planners. A controversial 'super sewer' is to be built instead. The Thames Tideway Tunnel will be fifteen miles long, cost £4.2 billion and take seven years to complete once work begins in 2016. Thames Water and the government insist the tunnel is essential: the city's Victorian drains cannot cope, and the new sewer will stop such vast quantities of waste flooding into the River. But several local councils and environmental groups oppose the project, arguing that cheaper, less disruptive alternatives exist.[87] It's right that we're willing to spend serious amounts of public money protecting our natural environment, but the question in this instance seems to be whether the super sewer is sticking plaster or cure.

London is scored with lost rivers like the Fleet, waterways that have been culverted out of sight and turned into sewers. But, under everything we have thrown over, around and into them, they still irresistibly run down to the Thames; their force has been curtailed but it is still just about intact. London has also lost several entirely man-made canals. They may have been ambitious projects in their day but they were never natural and so, when they disappeared, they were gone for good, drained and filled in.

I often think of these lost navigations and how brilliant it would be if they were still around. Imagine if it were possible to cruise from Rotherhithe to Peckham or from Croydon to New Cross, from Pimlico up to Victoria or from Kensington High Street down to Chelsea Creek. I decide to find them all, to pace out their lost routes on foot, searching for their clues and their ghosts. It takes a few days and wears huge holes in two pairs of socks.

The Grand Surrey Canal and Croydon Canal were the furthest reaching of the old canals and, if they had survived, would open up south-east London to boats. It's an approximation, but the route of the Overground line from Rotherhithe to West Croydon is a hint of the area these two connected cuts covered. Certain tracks run exactly where water once did, and the station at West Croydon sits on an infilled canal basin. Both the Grand Surrey and the Croydon Canals are long lost but fragments remain. Two tiny flashes of the Croydon Canal live on as ponds and, if artefacts like mooring bollards and heavy chains can be called 'poor man's sculpture' (Eric de Maré), tracing the route of the Grand Surrey is a little like following a sculpture trail.

As I follow the Surrey's route north from Peckham Library on foot, the first sign of its former existence is a one-kilometre-long narrow park named after the waterway. If you have canals on your mind, the concrete path cutting between grassy banks here immediately recalls one. Two black and gold cast-iron bridges, still with their towing paths intact, complete the illusion. Gritty wet barge ropes have worn deep, finger-width grooves into the bridges' stone walls.

Additional clues that mark out the canal's route to the Thames include a marooned and increasingly ruinous red and black latticed footbridge in Burgess Park, and a colourful but fading mural in the Friary Estate, depicting an annual Canal Bridge Green Fayre. A road sign at the top of Peckham Park Road reads 'Canal Bridge', and down a discreet alley at the side of a PC World are the very pretty and utterly anomalous cottages of 1–9 Canal Grove. The lost canal continues north from here, first through industrial estates, then densely packed housing, around Millwall Football Club, past the old Deptford Borough Council Slipper Baths and on to Surrey Canal Road. The junction with Mercury Way marks the spot where the Croydon Canal would once have met the Grand Surrey. A lone mooring bollard sits by a bridge. Huge painted letters spell out the names of Bridge and Victoria Wharves.

Further north, Windlass Place and an old Greater London Council map of the Pepys Estate reveal that a canal once passed this way. An invisible border is crossed just beyond the estate; suddenly the blocks of flats I'm walking past are shiny and new. In Russia Dock Woodland, iron mooring bollards line the path and short lengths of chunky black chain lie low in the leaves and the grass. The exact spot the canal would have kicked out into the Thames is hidden but reachable, a small inlet surrounded by expensive riverside flats. I arrive, legs aching, at low tide; the canal mouth is muddy by the river edge, sandy further in.

Work was authorised to begin on the Grand Surrey in 1801, with navvies digging south from Rotherhithe and finishing up in Peckham 25 years later. The slow progress and modest distance covered were not due to the terrain but to various business wrangles and land ownership issues behind the scenes. It opened in stages from 1807, lined with kilns and sawmills, and serviced by barges carrying timber and lime. *The Canals of South and South East England* by Charles Hadfield explains that the Grand Surrey's ambitious but never realised route was intended to be from the Thames at Rotherhithe to Mitcham, by way of Camberwell, Kennington, Clapham and Tooting, with branches to Deptford, Peckham, Borough and Vauxhall. Proposals to link to Greenwich and Elephant and Castle also floated around, plus a connection with the Kennet & Avon Canal at Reading. Locals would use the relatively short section of waterway that was built to fish and row, and there was even illegal dog racing on the towpath. *London's Lost Rivers* reveals that by 1811, 'the canal was so popular with illicit traders that bank rangers were appointed to maintain order'. Commercially it was much less of a success, although its disappearing act lasted decades. The defunct Camberwell Branch was finally drained in 1974 because of a fear that people would fall in and drown.

The 34-foot-wide Croydon Canal opened a couple of years after the Grand Surrey, in 1809, and, despite initial ambitions to reach all the way to Portsmouth, it stretched south from New Cross for just nine-and-a-quarter miles. According to Hadfield, 'The canal carried stone, lime, fuller's earth and timber from Croydon and brought coal and general merchandise back.' Two mighty forces killed it off within a few years. The first was geography. The landscape it cut through was deeply challenging for both engineers and bargees, rising as it did 167 feet above sea level. An eye-watering 26 locks were required for the two-and-a-half miles between New Cross and Forest Hill, and the ensuing tailbacks of boats were notorious. Although this landscape was terrible for journey times, it made the canal popular with pleasure-seekers, who would paddle along its waters and picnic on its picturesque banks. The second killer was

the railways. The Croydon Canal was sold to the London &
Croydon Railway in the 1830s. Hadfield quotes an amusing
poem from a book called *Stray Leaves from the Scrapbook of
an Awkward Man* by F. Slous (1834), which describes, in
verse, 'A Dialogue between the Croydon Railroad and the
Croydon Canal':

> Then spake the Canal, – Thou worst of my foes,
> Dost taunt my misfortunes and brag to my nose;
> Base, rascally railroad, my tears were thy laughter.
> Like surgeons, you bought me, to cut me up after.

The industrial artefacts like bollards and bridges that allow
the lost canal hunter to join the dots of the Grand Surrey's
route don't remain for the Croydon Canal but, unlike the
Surrey, the actual waterway hasn't been completely filled
in. Two short stumps of water remain – one in a public
park and one in a nature reserve. Both leftovers act as valuable wildlife habitats as well as springboards into the past.

The longest stump is at Betts Park in Anerley, close
to the Overground station. I walk from the station to the
park and find that the Croydon's current incarnation is as
an attractive, tree-lined pond with a distinctly canal-like
quality. A slender strip of water stretches along the park's
short western edge, with a towpath running alongside

it. It's particularly narrow, nowhere near as wide as the Regent's Canal or Grand Union. The water is fenced off. Low-rise flats overlook it on one side, large oaks and horse chestnuts on the other. Swathes of cow parsley bloom on the banks, tangled up with ivy. Moorhens busy themselves in the margins, mallards patrol about. The flat water is disturbed by upsurges of bubbles as aerators strain to prevent the short strip from stagnating.

Dacres Wood Nature Reserve is a fairly long walk north of Betts Park, tucked away down Catling Close, a dead-end street marked as a private road. It's a much smaller section of canal and easy to miss. On the day I visit it is also locked up. Happily the water is right beside the gate and I can see it from the road. The canal has truly become pond here. The air rings with bird song, the foliage is dense and an especially lustrous green, thick reed bed surrounds the water edges and there's little reason to think it was ever a working cut. It's a shame it's locked up, but it's pristine as a result; there is no litter or vandalism and the wildlife is left to its own devices. Just peering at it over the fence feels like an act of trespass.

The lost canals south of the River traced, I turn my attention to the other side of London and the north bank of the Thames. The Grosvenor and Kensington Canals once allowed barges into the comparatively flat heartlands of west London. Built in 1825, the Grosvenor was the capital's shortest canal, running north from the Thames at Chelsea Bridge to what is now Victoria Station. It began its working life as early as 1725, when a tidal channel was used to serve the riverside Chelsea Waterworks Company. It was canalised and extended to aid the development of Belgravia, with wharves built along its route for timber, coal and stone. It was gradually infilled as the railways developed. As well as being the shortest and oldest of the lost canals, the Grosvenor can also claim to have operated commercially for the longest. Its much truncated length was still being used by rubbish barges into the late 1990s.

The Kensington Canal has similar roots – it serviced the Lots Road Power Station at Chelsea Creek and followed the course of an existing waterway, although one more substantial than a tidal channel. Counter's Creek was a proper river, a Thames tributary that rose in Kensal Green and formed the boundary between Kensington and Fulham. The border between the two boroughs is a good way of imagining the Creek's course today. The natural river was eventually culverted, and the canalised stretch between Lots Road and Kensington High Street infilled and covered by rail tracks. Parts of the Grosvenor and Kensington Canals remain by the Thames, where both are being resurrected as focal points of exclusive residential developments.

I arrive at Victoria Station, planning to trace the route of the Grosvenor Canal from the station down to Chelsea Bridge, and then to walk further west to find what remains of the Kensington. There are a series of bridges heading south along Buckingham Palace Road. They pass over wide rail tracks which, at a push, it's possible to imagine were once water. The Ebury Bridge Estate was built over the infilled canal here, and the faint trace of a canal bridge remains, its arch fossilised within a white-washed brick wall. Buddleia bursts from the entombed hump, as it does from every other urban canal bridge.

It's a short walk from the estate to the new Grosvenor Waterside development. I get my first glimpse of water just where Chelsea Bridge Road meets Grosvenor Road. It's low tide and Canada geese and mallards are sleeping on a small beach of white shale. Mysteriously, there is no mud. White lock gates with steering wheels mark the entrance to the canal, with a rule up the side suggesting that, at high tide, the water can reach a depth of eighteen feet. The canal here has become a water feature, cutting between otherwise blank, if smart, residential blocks. Grosvenor Waterside is rich in Eric de Maré's poor man's sculpture: three sets of locks to keep the tide out, cast-iron mooring bollards and rings, heavy timber beams, neat semi-circle footholds cut into the canal sides to act as ladders. All are perfectly kept heritage features but workaday ones, at odds with their luxurious new surroundings; a one bedroom apartment here costs £875,000.[88]

I walk west along the Thames for a while, past Battersea Park on the opposite bank and the giant chalet-style house-boats of the Chelsea Yacht and Boat Company on this one, but at World's End I am pushed away from the water. Lots Road, with its terraced town houses, runs parallel to the River but the water is hidden from view and out of reach. Lots Road Power Station sits on this street, derelict but now at the heart of a redevelopment project. It's currently a work in progress, hidden behind high-gloss hoardings. Lots Road leads up to Chelsea Harbour and another hous-ing development around Imperial Wharf Station. There's still no public access to the Thames. It doesn't seem right that private projects are allowed to steal the water away like this, not just blocking it from view but also making it impossible to walk up to or alongside. Who exactly does the River belong to anyway?

At the western end of Lots Road there is a brilliant view from a road bridge of the old Kensington Canal. It's tidal – one of the reasons it was quickly a commercial failure

– and when the tide is out as it is right now, the stub is empty, its high-ribbed, weed-slicked concrete walls completely exposed. There are no water birds enjoying the intertidal mud here, only masses of litter. Dumped traffic cones list on the slimy green canal bed among tyres, bottles, cables, crates, cans, pipes and various other unidentifiable pieces of plastic. It's detritus that has washed in on the tide and been flung off this bridge. Londoners profess to love water, we say blue landscapes in cities make us feel brighter and healthier, but we continue to treat our waterways with disdain. Things may not be as bad as they were in the days of the Fleet, but during a single sunny day on the Regent's Canal, in a single spot, I can watch someone chuck in a glass bottle, fling a cigarette butt off a balcony and even urinate straight into the water. The butts from the balconies are especially astounding, as they come from the very people who have paid over the odds for a home with canal views.

The Kensington Canal follows the Overground line between Imperial Wharf and West Brompton stations so I trace the first part of its route by train. The tracks cut low between tall brick walls and thick herb banks. It's easy to recast these rail tracks as water and the passing platforms as towing paths. Back on foot, I walk along the top edge of Brompton Cemetery, visible from the road through high arched windows built into tall Victorian walls. The view is of old gravestones swimming in a peaceful blue haze of forget-me-nots. I head north up Warwick Road to Kensington High Street. The canal basin sat just south of here. Another housing development is in progress, in its early stages, so the space, for now, feels as open and industrial as the basin once might.

The Grand Surrey, Croydon, Grosvenor and Kensington Canals were all designed to connect with the Thames, and ultimately the ocean. The final lost canal I seek out, the Cumberland Spur, had humbler reasons for existing. Built in 1830, it branched off the Regent's Canal in Camden town and cut for 800 metres towards Euston. It serviced an agricultural market and military barracks with stone, hay, ice and food, as well as ammunition and livestock. It was decommissioned after the Second World War and infilled with rubble from the Blitz. Today, a red and gold, three-storey floating pagoda – a Chinese restaurant – marks the spot where the Cumberland Spur began and, a few metres away, Gloucester Gate Bridge passes over what once was water.

The Cumberland's route is best imagined as Albany Street, which, incidentally, is where my first flat in London was after university halls. It was a privileged place to live in hindsight – a low-rise block of old council flats close to Regent's Park – but it was a long time ago, before rents went through the roof. I lived on this street for two years and had absolutely no idea there was once a cut running right behind it. The Regent's Canal makes an abrupt 90 degree turn just east of the zoo, determinedly heading away from the park (and from Albany Street) and into Camden. The Spur continued to follow the edge of the park. A nub remains, now a shady private mooring for a handful of narrowboats.

I visit on a late afternoon of sunbursts, tropical downpours and violent gusts, on a day when the area rolls with a green and white blanket of late-blooming cow parsley. Standing on Gloucester Gate Bridge, it now seems obvious there was once a waterway here, where before it never did. I have crossed this funny bridge so many times thinking it a folly, not evidence of a watery past. Now I see that the gardens of Park Village East sit in a gully that is clearly canal shaped. If the Spur had somehow survived, we would be able to cruise past these canal-side villas and moor up right outside my first flat.

12. truth, illusion

A heatwave hits. The air inside the boat has become a solid, cloying thing that has to be waded through. Outside, her steel shell grows hot enough to sear bare skin. We sweat and sigh and mooch about. On days as humid as this one, we lounge on deck, loosely watching, or sprawl inside and listen. London is undone by the heat, inhibitions have burned up and drifted off. The Cut echoes with drunken yelps, sun-pink poseurs slide around in blow-up dinghies, the disco barge paces east and west seeking someone to thrill. King's Cross has become a destination in its own right, no longer just a terminus, and the area around the canal is particularly popular. The towpath couldn't be busier. Hot weather draws people to the water but the weed-coated Cut offers little relief. It sits there dormant, a crowded, steaming slick.

Just as the inside of a canal boat can plunge to far icier temperatures in winter than a house or a flat ever would, in summer it can get far hotter. While it's relatively easy to warm a cold boat up if you have the fuel, it's a lot harder to cool a hot boat down. Return home after a day away, when the metal boat has been sealed shut in full sun for several hours, and the interior will be like an oven. We will throw everything open as soon as we get back, but it takes a long time for the stored heat to dissipate. If we're in, we hook open the front and rear doors, and the large side hatch. The windows only open a fraction, but that fraction helps, and we drape the glass with gauzy sarongs to shut the sun and the insects out. The flies that do get through are trapped by our many resident spiders, who have taken to weaving elaborate nets over the windows and the front and rear decks. The heat seems to increase their productivity, not dampen it like it does ours.

Long sunny days on board may be stifling but they mean electricity is much easier to generate. In summer we can rely solely on our solar panels to fully charge the boat's batteries, and in turn power the lights, water pumps and even the tinny inbuilt car stereo. Most of all, we rely on them to run the twelve-volt refrigerator and its icebox. In winter fresh food can be kept cool in a kitchen cupboard; in the summer it will start to cook of its own accord if it's left out. The fridge groans and grinds and shakes about as it puts everything it's got into keeping food cold. Its efforts eat up most of our solar energy, but mean we can have choc ices and cold beer whenever we like.

The boat is currently tied up opposite a small nature reserve and beside a gloriously crumbling old brick warehouse that is embedded with mysterious chains and hooks. This building is destined to become restaurants and shops. In a few months mooring here will be banned as the conversion takes hold, and whether boats will be allowed back remains unclear. The whole of King's Cross is being redeveloped at the moment. The vision for it is sensitive to the area's built heritage, but there are always people who lose out when developers sweep in. For now, it seems almost fantastical to moor amid one of Europe's largest building sites, a construction project that, despite being unfinished, is still full of people, living, working, arriving, departing. Every few minutes trains tunnel under the canal out of King's Cross and over it from St Pancras. I could lie in bed all day listening to station announcements direct and reassure, or call Inspector Sands urgently to the operations room, if only it wasn't so hot. Instead we retreat to the shadier parts of the new King's Cross.

The metamorphosis is heart-stopping. This tract of land behind the stations and between the tracks is becoming remarkably polished; King's Cross St Pancras has got itself a persuasive new personality. All around, thrusting high-rises are shooting up, glass office blocks to the south, luxury flats to the north. The new gods are set to move in – Facebook at Euston, Google at King's Cross. Fashionable new places to eat and drink open daily. The area – which contains within it more than twenty historical buildings, three of which are Grade I listed – is being groomed into something modern but mercantile, smart but humane. The canal cuts right through the middle of it all and is crucial in creating this effect, not just because of its industrial history and surviving warehouses and wharves, but because people love water; it draws them in and creates a sense of community on its banks. The Cut and its boat and animal life bring an authenticity that newly developed cityscapes often lack.

The Granary Building and Granary Square are the focal point; the building's conversion into an art school and eateries is undoubtedly majestic, and the new square is thronged at this time of year, the visiting public policed at all times by private security guards in jaunty baseball caps. At its heart is a fountain, which on a hot day is full of kids in just their pants, running in and out of the water jets, whooping. At night, the fountain is lit up all the colours of the rainbow. Giant AstroTurfed steps run down from the square to the canal and are packed with picnickers during the day, drinkers in the evening. Last weekend the Floating Cinema hooked up an open-air screen opposite the steps and played old horror films every night. We could watch from the roof of our boat.

It is fun to be in the thick of it for a couple of weeks, but it's also odd to live in such a fitful, half-finished land-scape. Our squat, slow boat seems to shrink here. Inside Pike everything's the same, outside all is a race and a rush, a tidal wave of new. I find I am starting to prefer King's Cross late at night, when it has cooled down, emptied out and the special effects have been switched off; when everything is paused and we can have the work in progress to ourselves.

— ◆◆◆ —

I rent a desk in a studio in north London and haunt a few libraries in town, but sometimes I stay at home to work, especially if the weather is good and lunch breaks can be taken with my plants on the roof. This morning I am in the kitchen procrastinating over coffee when a pair of men approach, two dark shapes that I watch moving closer through the half-open slats of the blind. They stop in front of the window, centimetres from the glass and from me. One of the men leans over onto the boat and, in my position at the kitchen sink, I find I am now occupying the space under his armpit. This happens a lot and I hate it. I know we have parked ourselves on a public waterway adjacent to a public path – and long may this continue – but Pike isn't street furniture to be leaned upon.

Canal boats in London are as common as park benches. They prove fascinating to some people, an aberration to others. There's something of the zoo about the Cut and I think boaters can be regarded by some passers-by as other than human. Complete strangers will stroll by and ask if they can get on board to have a closer look. We always say yes but insist on a guided tour of their home first. And there are the creeps who throw things at the boat – stones, bottles and other missiles that could easily smash a window. They're bored and we're an easy target. From inside the boat, especially in summer when everything is open, I often hear snatches of towpath heart-to-hearts, telephone conversations, sometimes discussions about the boat and our imagined life. It's incredible how many people get the urge to touch Pike, to give her a slap or a push. At best I'm a forgotten observer and at worst a spy, watching and listening behind a camouflage of steel and twitching lace. The noises can be worrying – raised voices close at hand or thuds overhead. The hatch in the living room opens wide and allows us to investigate without the leaving the boat, but we're regularly dragged out on deck or up onto the roof by a puzzling sound we can't quite place. The culprits have ranged from a pigeon, a cat and a trapped bottle of beer to a tourist and a thief. More often than not it's flights of fancy and thin air.

The conversation outside the kitchen window becomes more and more animated. The leaning man suddenly stands bolt upright and starts punching the boat. It's not the first time someone has taken their rage out on Pike while I quiver silently inside, debating how best to react. Since it's broad daylight I feel I should do something, instead of just hoping they go away. The men start to move off and I stick my head out of the front door, thinking a glimpse of me will effectively let them know that this boat is a home not a punch bag. They explode at the provocation, screaming at me for daring to tell them what to do. I haven't actually said anything. They stalk off angry and I stand there pathetic. I quietly close the door, walk into the living room and weep.

I feel exposed on the boat and closer to a London I don't like. While I am certain that the Cut is a safer place than it once was, a string of violent break-ins on boats, towpath muggings and a decent amount of our own paranoia have pushed us to gate ourselves behind powder-coated steel bars. We've moored in places where the fear of getting robbed means we've felt forced to babysit Pike rather than go out at night. There's a secluded, unlit stretch of towpath by Victoria Park and the Hertford Union that is becoming notorious. I had never called the police before, but I've called them several times since we started cruising. I have become one of those people who complains about 'antisocial behaviour'. This doesn't make me feel good. Unpleasant things don't happen regularly, but they happen often enough, and I admit I get the night fears a lot. What makes me seethe the most is when people jump on the boat's roof. One young man was terribly apologetic after I caught him attempting to steal our lifebuoy at three o'clock in the morning but clearly had no concept of how it might feel to be woken up by heavy footsteps overhead. Much worse things have happened to other people, and I count myself lucky that so far we've only attracted the attention of drunks and bored kids.

The night noises we contend with are ones peculiar to living on the water. For the uninitiated, they can keep you up, eyes wide at every thump, slap and creak as the boat shifts and bumps. It has taken time but we can now place each one and know what we need to worry about and what we do not – duck bills drumming on the steel as the birds forage through the weeds that cling to Pike, or geese raucously exploring the rooftop, versus a human up to no good. When it's quiet here we can hear trains moving through the tunnels beneath us. At first it sounded worryingly like a repetitive drip but now we can recognise the distant rattle of wheels on a track. I can fall asleep to the Cut's bass and bubbles, beaks and froth, but one ear is always alert to anything out of place.

Is the truth about somewhere its face when it's early or late, light or dark, foul or fair? Its modern incarnation or its mercantile past? There are so many possible interpretations of a landscape, and each person's verdict on it will vary. The characters within a place change it too. Virginia Woolf plays with the ability of a river and a row of houses to be more than one thing from one moment to the next in *A Room of One's Own*:

> What was the truth about these houses, for example, dim and festive now with their red windows in the dusk, but raw and red and squalid, with their sweets and bootlaces, at nine o'clock in the morning? And the willows and the river and the gardens that run down to the river, vague now with the mist stealing over them, but gold and red in the sunlight – which was the truth, which was the illusion about them?[89]

I think the answer is probably neither, or both. Truth and

illusion are as capricious as the view, and the viewer. I still can't quite grasp hold of the Cut, or work out where we fit within it, unfixed as we are. The landscape continues to be both threatening and benign, consistently split. On the boat, on the canal, I feel like we are more subject to London's fluid moods, her ill winds and her euphorics. Never have I felt so at home or so afraid.

Author Penelope Fitzgerald understood how these contradictory feelings can feed each other, and be addictive. A dash of danger makes home a more compelling place to be. Her Booker Prize-winning novel *Offshore*, first published in 1979, is about a community of barge dwellers living at Battersea Reach in the early 1960s and is based on her own experiences living on a leaky boat on the Thames. The River changes with the tides and the time of day; dawn is its most 'elusive hour'. As night subtly begins to shed its skin, 'darkness lifts off darkness, and from one minute to another the shadows declare themselves as houses or as craft at anchor'. The bargees, whose ageing boats are permanently moored and don't move, other than to sink fatally into the mud, are caught between not wholly belonging to firm land nor to the water; the shifting riverscape underlines their unstable position. Fitzgerald described the 'emotional restlessness' of her characters, explaining they are 'caught halfway between the need for security and the doubtful attraction of danger'.[90]

The thing that, for me, represents the truth about King's Cross more than anything else, and makes mooring here a pleasure, is the wildness that somehow manages to thrive in one tiny, sacred spot. Camley Street Natural Park sits on the site of a Victorian coal drop, sandwiched between the Cut and St Pancras Station. The drop allowed coal to be transferred from train to canal boat, cart or lorry so it could travel onward to multiple destinations around town. The site's dirty working days long over, it has now been a London Wildlife Trust nature reserve for 30 years. It interweaves with the canal, expanding out into the water with floating platforms and reed beds. The reserve even has its own barge moored by St Pancras Lock, home to a floating forest garden of fruit trees, bushes and herbs.

Coal, of course, fuelled the Industrial Revolution. Between 1860 and 1900 the number of miners working down pits in Britain increased from 307,000 to 820,000, and annual coal production soared from 80 million tonnes to over 225 million.[91] But the turn of the century saw the beginning of coal's decline, and pit closures came thick and fast after the Second World War. Once coal no longer needed to be dropped at St Pancras, the canal-side site was abandoned and left to run wild. By the mid-1970s, the drop had been demolished, leaving behind a wasteland where prostitutes serviced clients in little huts amid a rampage of buddleia, butterflies and rubbish. In 1981, the fly-tipped site was earmarked to become a coach park.

An inquisitive student, who was researching urban growing projects for her master's degree, stumbled upon the sordid spot after first trespassing onto the towpath, which was still kept locked, and then peeling back the fence to steal into the derelict site. As she explored the knotty abandonment, she felt a tingle that she couldn't ignore. She pursued it, with other campaigners and supported by the recently founded London Wildlife Trust, until the coach park idea was shelved and Camley Street Natural Park born. They took some convincing but the Greater London Council (GLC) had the imagination to overturn the site's land use designation and invite London Wildlife Trust to manage it as a nature reserve instead. Looking back at old photographs in the Trust's library from the 1930s, 1950s and 1980s, up to today, the transformation from coal drop – busy with horses and boats – through rubbish tip to fully fledged nature reserve is almost hard to believe. Camley Street's creation was a landmark step for urban nature conservation in Britain. It is living proof that it's possible to create a nature reserve from scratch in the middle of a city.

When it was officially opened in 1985 by the then leader of the GLC Ken Livingstone, the park was a sparse site in an area that was widely seen as undesirable. It had a chalet-style wooden hut of a classroom (an otherwise unwanted cricket pavilion), a large but still bare pond, a few saplings, a new fence and some magnificent entrance gates acquired from around St Pancras. Today it is an intricate jungle of water, marsh, meadow and woodland that seems as phenomenal as ever in comparison to its now smartened-up surroundings. Wandering the park's narrow paths, with plants skimming over shoulders and trees canopying protectively overhead, it feels far larger than two acres. Thousands of inner-city kids have passed through its tall iron gates, many experiencing nature up close for the first time. The Mayor of London's 2002 Biodiversity Strategy celebrates Camley Street Natural Park as an inspiration, one that has 'become a hub of communal and educational activity, supporting wildlife such as the reed warbler in a place where this would otherwise be unthinkable'.[92]

The site was designated a statutory nature reserve in 1986. Despite this, just a few years later it emerged that HS1 – the Channel Tunnel Rail Link – was destined to trample straight through it. The threat from the high-speed line was successfully fought off, and trains to Kent and the Continent now pass to the west of the reserve. That the natural park is an asset should be obvious to anyone, and the recent development project focused around Granary Square, which began in 2008, has more or less embraced it with vigour. There are plans for a footbridge that will allow people to cross over the Cut and the park between Camley Street and the new King's Cross. The park's future seems secure, if an awful lot busier.

The proximity of the canal has always been important. In *The Potential for Wildlife Habitats Along the Regent's Canal in Camden*, a London Wildlife Trust report published in 1983, Jacqui Stearn – who, it turns out, was that trespassing young MA student – draws out the intimate connections between people and plants that are possible in the landscape. 'The canal in Camden is a rich assemblage of plant and animal communities,' she writes. 'The barge people used towpath herbs to cure their horses and today people pick blackberries on the towpath banks.' Stearn had, by the time of writing the report, become Camley Street Natural Park's first warden.

Published ten years later, *Nature Conservation in Camden, Ecology Handbook 24* underlines the Cut's ongoing ability to connect people and wildlife: 'The canal's popularity makes it one of the Borough's best-used sites for the appreciation of nature'; it is a 'landscape feature of strategic import-ance'. Today, Camley Street Natural Park is a reservoir of wildness that feeds directly into the canal system, and the Regent's Canal continues to be a highway for nature as well as everything else. Cut and Camley combined are a force for good. We moor here and are neighbours with herons and dragonflies, warblers, buntings and bats.

The weather continues sticky and hot. Sunset offers some respite and brings out dark, fast-flitting shadows, tiny tricks of the light. The bats we see here are likely to be com-mon pipistrelles, Europe's smallest, hawking on the wing. The canal is both an important flyway and a rich foraging ground – the narrow, linear structure provides bats with a clear route to commute along using sound pulses, and the standing water attracts the crepuscular insects they like to eat. According to the London Bat Group, a single pipi-strelle will eat up to 3,000 midges, caddis flies, mosquitoes and other similar small insects in a night.[93] The creatures dart about in the soupy city light, drawing out figures of eight just above the boat and entertaining us well into the small hours. It seems King's Cross's true attractions are to be found right here on the Cut, with its many moods, its natural park and its dancing pipistrelle bats.

13. outside edges

It's time to move on. We set out around half past nine, heading west. The morning is bright, warm and still. A little cloudy. St Pancras lock is set low in our favour and three Welsh gents travelling east kindly help us in, up and out. A cormorant surfaces from a dive just ahead of us, a good omen from the water gods, sent to calm my move day nerves. (Why can't I be calmer?) Cormorants swam with us for long stretches during our maiden voyage and it's pleasing to have one with us early on today. Our aim is to get through Camden's run of three successive locks before the inevitable crowds accumulate.

The cormorant is traditionally 'a creature of ill omen', one onto which humans have long projected a 'sinister Gothic character', according to *Birds Britannica*. John Milton best crystallised our superstitions about the bird. In his epic poem *Paradise Lost*, Satan famously disguises himself as a cormorant and sits upon the tree of life 'devising death'. The bird's dark, stark silhouette has the power to unnerve, to put us on guard against bad luck, or worse.

Happily, the reputation-saving R.S.R. Fitter points out in *London's Birds* that when two wild cormorants frequented the top of Big Ben in June 1928, not only did no disaster befall the country, but England retained the Ashes the following winter. Perhaps my idea that the cormorant might be a creature of good fortune isn't so perverse.

Whether a predictor of good luck or bad, the cormorant is a striking sight on the Cut. The bird is what Adam Nicolson calls in his book *Sea Room: An Island Life in the Hebrides*, 'scandal and poetry, chaos and individual rage, archaic, ancient beyond any sense of ancientness'.[94] To have such a creature in a city, this gaunt totem of wild island life, is incredible. Every time I see one I gulp.

The cormorant is not pretty, gentle or soft. Not some tame goose, rail or duck. It is angular, aloof. It perches, indeed gothic, on exposed edges. The bird slips through the water, its back almost awash, then, fish-like, it dives and disappears. I've never seen what a cormorant looks like underwater, the canal is far too murky for that, but I trust *Birds Britannica* when it says, 'swimming cormorants are a curious blend of serpentine grace and clown's feet'. Artful and artless. And then the bird is undone, soaked through, and must hang itself out to dry. This lack of waterproofing means cormorants can dive to greater depths, a feature that's not useful in a shallow navigation like the Regent's Canal but much more so in the Thames or out at sea.

Jonathan Rosen's essay 'Because it's ugly' – which reviews *The Double-Crested Cormorant: Plight of a Feathered Pariah* by Linda Wires for the *London Review of Books* – has some of the best descriptions of the bird I have found. Rosen's love of the cormorant feels close to my own, stemming as it does from some amateurish urban birdwatching, in his case in New York. Most graceful underwater where it is least observed, by the time Rosen sees it on the rocks in Central Park the cormorant is 'a broken umbrella poking out of a bin after a shower on a windy day'. It is the bird's odd but eye-catching looks that make it so appealing. As Rosen says: 'the ancient fish-eaters [don't] have the colour and elegance of songbirds, but like silent movie stars they [have] faces'.

The cormorant is large and black, an oil-slick kind of black with metallic sheens in it that range from bronze and green to indigo and purple. It has bright white and yellow cheeks, an elastic throat pouch – like a pelican but much smaller – and a hinged, hooked beak. Its tail is broad and its large feet webbed. It has an emerald eye and 'frosty throat plumes'.[95] Naturalists have long argued that the cormorant is 'remarkably handsome'.[96] And agile. In *The Devil's Cormorant*, Richard J. King celebrates the bird's 'quick, tight plummet underwater', riffing on Amy Clampitt's sonnet 'The Cormorant In Its Element', which describes the dive as a 'sleek involuted arabesque, a vertical turn on a dime'. Said to occasionally groan, growl and even cackle – whether swimming, perched or drying off – on the Cut, the cormorant is most often solitary and silent.

Historically, despite being dogged by eerie symbolism and superstition, humans' relationship with the cormorant has been close and practical. Chinese and Japanese fishermen worked alongside cormorants for thousands of years, employing the birds to catch fish for them. Inspired by this, King James I kept a cormorantry on the Thames at Westminster and appointed a Keeper of the Royal Cormorants.

Sadly our relationship with the bird today can be fraught, not because the bird is a portent of bad things to come but because of its hunting prowess. Anglers don't seem to see the irony in this. Cormorants fish to survive and catch only what they need to eat. Hobbyists do it for fun. I am not anti-fishing – although if we are killing other than to eat, it becomes a blood sport like any other – but I am against anyone who calls for a cull of fish-eating birds because they can't handle the competition. The vilification and bloody persecution of the cormorant is something that has been written about and condemned, widely, but continues with a vengeance. Ted Hughes, a keen angler, at least had some respect for his rival and, in observing the cormorant, saw his own ridiculousness reflected back. The fisherman – a mere 'stump' dressed in 'space-armour' – can only dream of the cormorant's skilfulness, the bird's 'fish-action', its ability to dissolve itself into a fish and in turn dissolve fish into itself.[97]

Today's cormorant dives and disappears and, as it does, a curved yellow missile flies off the bridge ahead, narrowly missing Pike's nose. Here we go. This would be the first time we have been attacked from a bridge as we cruise, but I have been braced for such an incident for months. But no, it's just someone mistaking the canal for a dustbin again. The missile is an uneaten banana that has failed some test, and the Cut continues to be a repository for unwanted things.

We pull up in front of Kentish Town Lock and I hop off to do the gates, helped by a volunteer lock-keeper, while S. holds Pike in to the bank. It's already busy – Camden's waters have a powerful allure, especially for tourists, stoners and drunks. The sun is higher and less hazy now, and the morning is stretching out and growing hot. There's a man in a shiny tracksuit top and brand new blue jeans fast asleep on his stomach in the soft earth edge of the towpath.

His arms are crossed into a pillow, his legs crossed too. He looks content, like it was a good night. He wakes as we wait for the lock to fill, glances over, does up his fly, turns and goes back to sleep.

We move on to Camden's second lock. There's no lock-keeper here to help, and the gates are stiff. They are always heavy and slow to shift but sometimes, if there's a build-up of debris in the water, they can be especially hard to open and close. Operating locks with an audience – which is always the case at Camden – makes a tough job worse, humiliating even. As a woman often accused of being skinny, I feel like I have something to prove at lock gates. It may appear unlikely to some, but I can of course operate a lock. On our maiden voyage I did over 30. The process is never fast. It can take around a quarter of an hour to get through a lock and, here, people who haven't asked if you mind will take your photograph as you do.

The first time we drove the boat through Camden was badly timed. We were heading east and arrived at the top lock at about eight o'clock on a summer's evening. There were hundreds and hundreds of people out enjoying the heat, all drinking, all with something to offer in the way of advice. If S. is driving, I will be the one to open and close the lock gates. Some of the lock-side drinkers just couldn't make sense of this division of labour and made some lewd comments about the only work women are good for. It is they who have made me hate cruising through Camden, and they who first taught me to expect casual sexism at locks. Although I have gradually learned that dealing with other people is all part of the boating performance, the gawping throng of gongoozlers that gathers on this, London's busiest section of towpath, has become quite monstrous in my mind. If we could avoid cruising through Camden we would, but there's only one canal cutting west.

We have had one positive experience here. It was a Sunday, possibly the worst day in terms of crowds, but it was cold and we arrived early, before nine o'clock. We were cruising east and passed down through all three locks with a tiny tugboat. It had overtaken us in Maida Vale but waited for us to catch up at the top lock, preparing it ready for our arrival. Pike is usually too wide to share locks but because the tug was so small we could squeeze in together. An extra pair of boating hands meant we got through all three locks a lot quicker than usual and, instead of harassment, there was camaraderie. And music. The tug-boater had his stereo turned up high. He struck me as a hardy, carefree soul; a man of mystery and few words, who wore flip-flops in winter because he liked to feel the wind between his toes.

Today, once we are through the middle lock, we chug on to the third and final one. There's another volunteer lock-keeper here, recruited by the Canal and River Trust to help boaters out during peak hours and to keep an eye on water levels. If the gates are left open the middle pound can drain away into an unnavigable puddle. More people are starting to gather now, hanging off the railings and asking lots of questions, curious about us and our boat.

We slide in, close the gates, wind the paddles up to let the water in and wait for it to slowly fill (the journey west is uphill). When it looks like the water is equal inside and outside the lock in our direction of travel, the lock-keeper and I try to open the gates. They won't shift. We push and pull but nothing. It's fundamental this time, not my own weakness. We work out that one of the paddles on the bottom gate is stuck and hasn't completely dropped. This means water is escaping into the pound below and preventing the lock from filling. We decide there must be something solid under the paddle that's preventing it from dropping any further. Conferring with the lock-keeper, who is cool as a cucumber throughout, S. tries very gently pushing the boat into the top gates to try to nudge them open. Nothing happens. He tries again. Still nothing. We are trapped. In Camden. S. tries again and again. The gates simply won't budge if the levels aren't equal. But eventually, after a few more nudges, the backwash the boat creates as it moves forwards and back shifts the debris from under the paddle, allowing it to drop all the way. The lock fills, the top gates open and we escape at long last.

After a sharp bend by the giant floating pagoda and the Cumberland Spur, the canal curves around the perimeter of Regent's Park, deep in a gully now, past caged mammals on one side and caged birds on the other. The aviary sits to our right, a set of geometric, see-through pyramids with thousands of exotic birds caught inside its nets. The starlings are a surprise. Are they meant to be in there or have they willingly exchanged freedom for a reliable source of food? London Zoo is an attractive place for small city creatures – a colony of well-fed house sparrows nests in the eaves of the zoo's clock tower, zipping in and out of the enclosures in brave pursuit of a free lunch.

Soon after the aviary is beautiful Blow-up Bridge, named after a barge explosion that happened underneath it in 1874. It's nothing like the cute little humpbacks we all associate with rural canal bridges; it's tall, proud, imposing. Built of brick, it is three-arched, with diamond lattice railings on top and ten fluted cast-iron columns underneath. The metalwork is painted smart gloss black. There are circular windows cut into the brick above the columns, as if someone, once, might have been lucky enough to live inside. From a distance the bridge is a solid, understated, industrial beauty; close up it is streaked with bird poo and caught inside a chicken wire brace. It has a high under-curve with neat arches between each stout column. Despite the impression it gives of great weight – all that cast iron and baked brick – the space beneath it is airy and light. The fact Blow-up is set within the most peaceful and leafy part of the Regent's Canal adds to its elegant aura. The Cut is every bit the sleepy backwater in this spot. Trees bend double to dip their branches into the water, and the bramble bushes are deep and thick.

This stretch is idyllic but brief, and lush banks are soon replaced by the clipped, landscaped gardens of the park's grandest properties, which sweep right down to the canal and are protected by armies of statues, guard dogs and CCTV. Mooring is prohibited. Warning signs remind passers-by that theirs is private property and you trespass at your peril. Despite wanting to be older, most of these park mansions were built less than 30 years ago.[98] We decide the faux-Classical buildings must belong to absent oligarchs, and that snipers are tracking us from the roofs.

Leaving the genteel environs of the park behind, we pass under two low, grey railway bridges, flanked on both sides by low-rise housing blocks. One bridge carries trains to and from Marylebone, the other Metropolitan line trains in and out of Baker Street. We spend a lot of time under low bridges like these ones, passing close enough to touch the big braille-like rivet bumps and to see right into the gloomy pigeon crofts. As we slip through the shadows we are watched by hundreds of tiny orange eyes. The birds are barely visible, tucked away in dark recesses, but over the engine we hear their gurgles and coos, and the slap of lavender-grey wings flapping on the spot.

In *Field Notes from a Hidden City*, Esther Woolfson, wise defender of urban areas' pariah species, writes wonderingly about our disdain for what she see as the 'angels of the streets'. Confronted with her fellow Aberdonians' fear and loathing of the feral pigeon, she muses at length about why we would ostracise these birds, with their history so tied up with our own and their phenomenal navigation skills. As Woolfson describes the pigeon's close connection to the dove, she regrets that city pigeons 'emerge from the confusion at a great disadvantage, bearing with them our every prejudice towards urban life'.

Why do we despise them so? A scraggy pigeon

floundering in the street – its chewed-up feet in a puddle of goodness-knows-what, its beak pecking manically at a mangled kebab – is a sad sort of mascot for anywhere to have. I think that, most of all, pigeons make us feel guilty. They are the downtrodden, the ignored. Maybe we should try and appreciate them more. London wouldn't be London without them.

The pigeon is tenacious and has an astounding ability to stomach anything – chips, fried chicken, pizza, peanuts, curry, sliced white. More impressive is the fact it can recognise gestures and facial features. *Birds Britannica* explains that a feral pigeon can single out an individual who has fed it two or three times before from a crowd of many other people. The book argues convincingly for the pigeon, just as Woolfson does, reminding us of the species' role as a messenger and a symbol of peace, and that its guano was once an important ingredient in fertiliser and explosives. Darwin kept and studied pigeons, and 26 of the birds have been awarded the Dickin Medal, the animal equivalent of the Victoria Cross. The avian encyclopaedia points out that 'No species has featured more often or has worked harder for us – metaphorically and literally – in art, religion or our daily lives. It is worth bearing in mind when you next stand in a city street with the humble bird itself at your feet.' I'm warm to the idea that feral pigeons deserve a bit more respect. I'm also realistic and find it hard to imagine many Londoners being persuaded to see them as anything other than pests.

Emerging from under these particular rail bridges, we feel smaller and lower down than ever, the canal now occupying a scrape between a high bank and an industrial plant. The way ahead is blocked by a tall wall, with a dark gape cut into it. It's a stretch of water that is usually only accessible by boat, the main towpath now passing high up on street, not canal, level. This sump hosts Lisson Grove private moorings, which would be enviable except for the fact they sit in the shadow of an enormous electricity substation, now owned by EDF. The siding was once home to Lodge Road Power Station. There have been houseboats here since the late sixties – the power station was demolished in 1972 – a time when living on a static barge on the Regent's Canal would have been considered bohemian in the extreme. The canal is wide, and it's now a home for about 50 narrowboats, mostly moored nose to the bank.

Through the Eyre's and then Maida Hill tunnels, we emerge at street level in Maida Vale, with Blomfield Road's gated moorings on our right. Under a baby blue and gold bridge labelled 'Regent's Canal 1', we reach Browning's Pool and Little Venice, with its island of weeping willows, its tufted ducks and tour boats. It is here that the Regent's and Grand Union Canals meet. White stuccoed mansions line leafy streets, where the thirsty roots of plane trees have made the tarmac erupt into enormous boils. This burst of prettiness surrounding the canal junction was christened 'Little Venice' in the 1950s, and the pool named after poet Robert Browning, who lived nearby the century before. The pool was not always so smart, and there's rumour it was once known locally as 'Rat Island'. Today it's posh and popular with tourists. It's not possible to moor here without special permission, so we continue our journey, choosing to venture into the Paddington Basin, a short L-shaped spur of water that branches off to the left.

It's thrilling to slip-slide through central London like this but what of that anaemic tidiness, that corporate creep I have bemoaned? It's in evidence in fits and starts along the Cut's length, but nowhere is it more vigorous than down this cul-de-sac. Both the towpath and the water-way are cramped by three wide and low-flying concrete relief roads, including the four-lane A404 or Westway, as we leave Little Venice. Like Orwell's northern canal, it is 'a world from which vegetation [has] been banished'. I find this brutalism weirdly preferable to what we find further along, where a monolithic redevelopment project

– Paddington Central, Sheldon Square – radiates out from the back of Paddington Station. All pale grey and glass, it looks as though someone has drained the blood out of the place. The towpath is wide with no soft landscaping apart from a few spindly trees, caged inside circular benches. The usual, identikit chain stores have arrived and clumped together unimaginatively.

The Basin itself – where the water is at its widest as it reaches its dead end – is the focal point of the redevelopment. The blocky, ten-storey wing of St Mary's Hospital, which has sat on the south side of the basin since 1987, is now dwarfed by the glassy towers of Merchant Square, a construction project that aims to make Paddington a 'destination neighbourhood' and will include the tallest building in Westminster. While London aches for affordable homes, developers design and build anodyne places like this, where a 547 square feet flat – smaller than Pike – costs £750,000.[99]

On a sunny weekday morning in the Basin, all is quiet. A couple of window cleaners zip down a sheer face of smoked glass, polishing the countless windows with which they have been blessed. Security men in cheerful lime green t-shirts stand around looking listless, their eyes tracking anyone who decides to wander through. It reminds me of Canary Wharf: the private guards, the sterile flashes of standing water. The construction won't be complete until 2018. For now – and perhaps then too – if the canal boats weren't here, the Basin would be characterless.

Even the boats aren't immune to the buffing. The Canal and River Trust has invited businesses to tender for two permanent trade moorings in the Basin. In November, we will learn that the independent, slightly scruffy but much-loved Word on the Water bookshop barge is out, a British Land coffee boat and floating 'welcome centre' awarded moorings in its place.[100] The Canal and River Trust also plans to install a fleet of eighteen business barges, which it will let out as offices.[101] The implication of all this additional commercial space – something that isn't exactly going to be lacking in Merchant Square with all of its six towers offering retail or office space – is surely fewer places for cruising boats to moor. It's a queer thing for the Canal and River Trust to do at a time when the need for mooring spaces is more acute than ever, and the London Assembly's Environment Committee has recommended that 'the Mayor should, in the next set of amendments to the London Plan, more fully reflect the residential value of London's waterways, and include a policy to increase the number of moorings'.[102]

I'm not a fan of the redevelopment but there are redeeming features that make mooring in Paddington worth doing every now and then. It's possible to avoid the Basin and moor on the lead-up to it instead; in fact you can moor outside the new entrance to the tube and trim your home-to-station journey down to three seconds flat. From here you can walk ten minutes quickly south through grand back streets and reach Hyde Park, the part where the grass is long and the old oaks particularly gnarly. Or walk for five minutes to the cosy Victoria pub, or three minutes to hectic Edgware Road.

We moor up in this strange spot outside the station, in a position by a bridge where discarded baggies float in puddles of pee and a used condom sags forlornly in the canal, proof that Paddington hasn't completely exorcised its grubby side. We learn that a perky little coffee cart will set up outside our bathroom window every weekday morning to serve commuters their hot drinks. We realise that the room across the water with the floor-to-ceiling windows is a meeting room, where a group of 30 or so people will gather each morning and try not to catch our eye. We discover that the other windows, the ones with the mirrored glass, allow us a view of both ourselves and of the towpath that we never usually get. Without leaving the boat, we can spy on people and determine whether the person giving us a little test push is a tourist or someone more sinister. We also find out that on weekend evenings the tube will spit out packs of revellers in fancy dress, cartoon characters who jump on boats for a lark.

London remains consistent in her inconsistencies. There is the bloodless Basin here and, a few metres up water, there is the extraordinary Puppet Barge, which it's especially easy to escape to on foot while we are moored outside Paddington station. I have spent a few years now, as a sometime theatre writer, trying to convince people that puppetry is a serious art form, one able to be as heart-wrenching, illuminating and challenging as any other type of theatre. A place that combines my love of puppetry and my love of the Cut is a rare thing indeed, and so naturally I am drawn to this converted 1930s Thames lighter barge, with its wide red and yellow striped awning and its multi-coloured bunting that flaps invitingly in the wind.

Although its status has happily risen rapidly in the post-*War Horse* world, puppetry still sometimes feels like an outsider's art, just as boating feels like an outsider's way of living. In London, being a boater immediately places you outside of the ordinary. In the theatre world, being a puppetry company casts you to the outer edges of the accepted. In puppetry, limiting yourself to work only with strings makes you highly unusual. And so the Puppet Barge, semi-itinerant in its floating venue and only producing shows using long-string marionettes, sits on the outside edge of everything.

A gangplank leads off the towpath and onto the front deck, and from here steep steps direct the visitor down into the small, dimly lit lobby that serves as a box office and café, and a kitchen and dining room for the puppeteers when the public aren't about. The boat's riveted insides have been painted deep red. A collapsible wooden roof extension gives the space enough headroom for 50 steeply tiered bench seats and for two marionette bridges out back. Hand-carved wooden puppets hang by their strings from the ceiling, and tiny portholes at water level let in thin shafts of light, which are shut behind heavy drapes during a show. When moored in Little Venice, the Puppet Barge generally programmes plays for children, and it would be easy to assume that what's on offer will be twee, end-of-the-pier stuff, designed to please the area's steady stream of tourists. That isn't the case. The barge – and its resident Movingstage Marionette Company – is averse to the insipid and the cute.

The first show I watch on board is *Red Riding Hood and the Wolf Who Tried to Eat Her*. In Deborah Jones' version of the well-known tale – and her first script for marionettes – the Wolf and Granny take centre stage. He is a complicated creature, in the midst of an existential crisis and, ulti-mately, on a journey of reform. She is a faded opera diva, retreating more and more into her glittering past. It is Wolf and Granny's frustrations and sadness that give the story its interest and depth, perhaps particularly for the adults in the audience. Using wooden, long-string marionettes on their signature six-feet-by-three-feet stage, Movingstage delicately unfurl Jones' layered story of love and loss.

The play begins with a twelve-inch-tall Red Riding Hood, in crushed velvet cape, twisting out her first wob-bly tooth. She determines to give it to her grandmother, because Granny has a gap in her own teeth that lets the wind whistle through and ruins her singing. The tooth fairy – a bored spirit called Stan, made of silver and glass – is unable to resist and whisks the tooth away. But even-tually he agrees to let Hood have it back as long as he can accompany her on a brave trip to Granny's cottage in the woods.

Red Riding Hood is feisty, with Robin Hood-style ambi-tions to become a highwayman who robs from the rich and gives to the poor. Encountering the Wolf for the first time, rather than being scared, she pities him, and resolves to make him happy. Hood's fearless kindness drives the Wolf wild.

The set is small in width but long in depth, allowing

for gauzy layers and good perspective. The protagonists are all marionettes but shadow and rod puppetry are used too. The production is atmospheric; the puppeteering nuanced and adept. In the end Red Riding Hood is blessed with two grannies, one losing her marbles and the other cross-dressing and distinctly wolfish.

I visit the Puppet Barge again in the week when *Red Riding Hood* has ended and the next show, *Brer Rabbit and the Tarbaby*, is in rehearsal. Director Rob Humphreys invites me over during a lunch break. We share a meal at a foldout table in the lobby and he tells me the story of the barge.

Rob's partner Kate is the daughter of its founders, Juliet and Gren Middleton. In the 1970s, Juliet was working at the Little Angel Theatre and Gren, an exile from South Africa, was in film, doing lighting and camera work. The couple wanted to set up their own theatre but couldn't afford to rent or buy a building. Inspired by the candlelit Magic Lantern Narrowboat and the knowledge that old Thames lighter barges were going for a song in the east, they decided they would convert a boat into a puppet theatre. They were offered the Maybrent for free if they agreed to fit her out, and therefore spend money, at Blackwall Dock. Lighter barges had once been tasked with transferring goods to and from moored, ocean-going vessels but as

London's docks closed, many were left redundant. Juliet and Gren's barge was 72 feet long and thirteen feet wide, and would fit snugly into London's canal locks.

The couple's maiden voyage took place at one o'clock on a cold January morning in 1982. They set out west from Blackwall as the tide was coming in, propelled along by an outboard motor and heading for the mouth of the Regent's Canal. They were expected at Limehouse, and someone was waiting on the bank to meet them. But disaster struck. The person on shore let go of the ropes and the barge was carried off by the tide, at speed, into town. The engine flooded and failed, and there was no radio to call for help. As the barge swept past the river police at Wapping, Gren managed to send out an SOS with a torch. Incredibly the police spotted the light signals, rescued them and towed the boat back to Limehouse.

The Puppet Barge opened its doors to audiences in Camden later that year. It was heated by two ranges and lit with gas lamps, and the inaugural play was *The Rime of the Ancient Mariner*. Mobile phones were available by then, and Rob doesn't think the Puppet Barge would have survived without theirs. Gren and Juliet attached their phone's aerial to a scaffold pole on the barge's roof and were able to run a box office from the boat. The couple staged marionette shows in Camden for two years, then moved the barge to Little Venice, where it has been mooring in Browning's Pool ever since.

The challenges of producing theatre afloat are many and ones any boater would recognise: it's hard work keeping the boat warm in winter and cool in summer, space is tight, black waste has to be stored on board and then disposed of, and drinking water is limited. The closest tap in Little Venice is three hosepipe lengths away. The backstage area is dark and cramped: puppeteers struggle to stand when on the marionette bridges and heads regularly crack against metal and wood. After welcoming audiences on board, checking tickets and showing people to their seats, the puppeteers leave by the front door and re-enter at the aft, climbing in through a hatch, down a vertical ladder of metal rungs, into the back cabin where they position themselves on one of the bridges ready for curtain up.

The Puppet Barge attracts a certain kind of puppeteer, nimble manipulators willing to accept the quirks of boat life. Every year it makes the two-day cruise west then south to Richmond, where it programmes shows aimed at adult audiences. To get under the bridges on route, the boat's wooden top has to be collapsed; it takes a day to take down and a day to put back up. The boat has a four-foot draught, which means it sits deeper in the water than the average canal boat. This can be problematic. Rob lists carpet, saris and endless plastic bags as items pulled out of its low-slung propeller. Maybrent has two berths and a stage as big as a bed, so the puppeteers will often live aboard during the summer season.

The barge makes its money from ticket sales and by renting out a few moorings in Richmond and King's Cross. It's a hands-on, family business, and one of very few arts venues in London that doesn't rely on funding or sponsorship to survive. Enter the Puppet Barge's world and find a great deal of warmth matched with a steely independence, self-sufficiency and pride. Rob argues convincingly for marionettes, insisting that this style of puppetry is able to express something other puppets cannot. The Puppet Barge is one of the only theatres in town still consistently producing shows with marionettes, and I sense he and his colleagues feel a deep responsibility to keep the strings alive.

I return to the barge to watch *Brer Rabbit*. I buy a home-printed programme for 30 pence and read inside that: 'there are emotions of tenderness and anger, gentle or strong, of love and hatred, painful or pleasing. The marionette is capable of moving the mind in any one of these directions.' The set is simple; tiny in reality but at points managing to evoke the sense of wide, open plains. It's populated, somewhat sparsely, by a beautifully carved menagerie of wooden animal puppets, including a nodding tortoise, a skeletal buzzard, an obese cicada and a curious brown bear. Brer Rabbit himself has lively ears that swivel and point, and Brer Fox a particularly expressive fur tail.

The Brer Rabbit stories – characterised by the triumph of mischievousness over malice – are thought to have their roots in both African and Native American cultures. It is likely that the stories travelled over to the southern states of America with slaves, where they could well have melded with Cherokee tales. The stories were popularised throughout the US by Joel Chandler Harris in the 1880s, and Enid Blyton retold them for children in the 1930s. Brer Rabbit may be small and weak, but his ingenuity means he can overcome bigger, stronger adversaries. On the Puppet Barge's tiny stage, a universal source of hope among oppressed peoples plays out: the rabbit represents the outsiders, taking on the powers-that-be and winning.

autumn

———◆———

metroland

Grand Union Canal
Paddington to Uxbridge

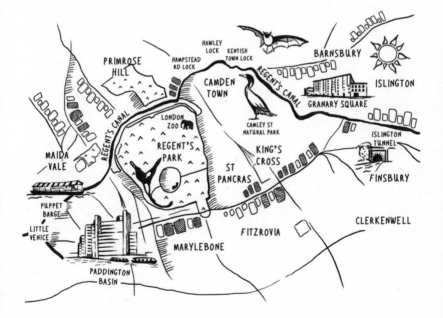

14. voyage out

I don't often spend time considering Pike's underparts or exactly how she manages to keep afloat, in much the same way few of us think about a building's foundations or how it stays standing up. We must have faith in such things if we want to sleep at night. The boat's ability to float is a given, one of those daily, unquestioned miracles that means life can continue in the way it always does.

The leak was an interruption, one that forced us to think about the space beneath the floorboards. Most of all it taught us that, over time, the cabin bilge at the bottom of the boat will fill up with gallons of water if we have poorly connected pipes. While I'm now conscious of the shallow cellar beneath us, and use our inspection hatches more regularly to make sure all is well down there, the hull itself – the outer part of Pike's shell that is always submerged – remains an unknown. Because a third of her bulk sits underwater, hidden from view, my sense of the boat's true shape and volume is skewed and short of what it actually is. If I do try to take a look, the Cut's mirror skin and the fringe of weed that rings Pike's waterline collude to prevent it.

The hull has been on our minds of late; it is due our attention. We last saw it, briefly, on the back of a lorry the day we bought the boat. Pike was heaved out of the water in Derbyshire and whisked off to Hertfordshire by road. It was one of the strangest and most stressful days of our lives. To see your home on the back of a truck all set to hurtle down the motorway is a sure way to put your heart in your mouth. But since she was dropped back into the water at Hemel Hempstead and life as we now know it began, the hull has been out of sight, and we have little idea how it is faring.

Every few years a steel boat needs to be taken out of the water so her hull can be cleaned, inspected and repainted. It's a process known as 'blacking', named after the bitumen used to coat the boat's bottom to protect it from wear and tear. Pike hasn't been blacked for six years, and so her re-blacking is long overdue. It's important we do it now, while the weather is still warm enough for the bitumen to dry.

We book a week in a dry dock in Uxbridge. We will do the cleaning and painting ourselves, and continue to live on Pike in the boatyard while we do. It's an important job, although, for now, something of a mystery. All we know for sure is that a properly protected hull is absolutely vital to staying afloat. If we mess this up, we sink.

To deal with the pressure, I make lists. Long lists. Lists of what to research, what to buy, what especially to worry about. We stock up on tinned goods like it's the last days before a disaster, and source hooded dust suits, face masks and disposable gloves. To get to Uxbridge from our current mooring in the Paddington Basin, we will follow the Paddington Branch of the Grand Union to its western limit at Bull's Bridge Junction, before joining the Grand Union proper heading north. It's about eighteen miles, through just one lock. In theory, it should take about eight hours to travel this distance, but we're giving ourselves three days so we can stop along the way. If we took the tube to Uxbridge it would take 45 minutes.

Our journey will take us through the inner edges of Metroland, that definitive suburban sweep that runs north-west along the Metropolitan line. It's a near-mythical place in my mind, made so by John Betjeman, whose partly rhyming ode to the area was filmed by the BBC in 1973 and interwoven with footage shot from a Metropolitan train in 1910, before the house building began.

We will set out from a point close to St John's Wood – Betjeman's 'sweet secret suburb on the city's rim', a 'forerunner of the suburbs yet to come', passing near to Neasden and Wembley, once able to be called an 'unimportant hamlet'. At Harrow our route will split off from Betjeman's, loosely following a branch line to Uxbridge. We will discover that Metroland by canal in 2014 is a place of light industry, depots, logistics and storage, of low-rise housing developments, oversized supermarkets, golf courses and car parks. A territory criss-crossed by the Metropolitan, Central and Piccadilly lines, and First Great Western tracks too. A place where bypasses and motorways are always close at hand, and aeroplanes always overhead.

The term 'Metroland' was first coined in 1915, used in brochures and on posters to promote a dream where slow country living was matched with fast rail connections into London. The commuter was being invented. Things have changed since then, and not just in terms of a comprehensive paving over of what once was green. Metroland was conceived at a time when ordinary people – manual workers and clerks – could expect to own a reasonably sized house with a garden, close to a station. A hundred years on, expectations in the South East have shifted somewhat.

It's late September by the time we set out, but it's beautifully sunny and still, perfect boating weather. As we slip through Little Venice, the water is high, or the towpath low; either way the canal looks like it might overspill its banks. We pass the roaring Westway – that 'massive concrete motion-sculpture' as J.G. Ballard calls it[103] – and alongside Meanwhile Gardens and the Trellick Tower. At Queen's Park there's a row of terraced, four-storey, yellow-brick houses that back right onto the water's edge. This brief stretch of Harrow Road is the only instance I know of in London where houses on land are so closely connected to the canal, where back doors open straight out onto water with no buffer in between. In my mind this is the true, if tiny, Little Venice.

We pass under Ladbroke Grove and the landscape changes instantly. The residential and commercial buildings we have passed since Paddington are replaced by train tracks, gasometers and vacant land on one side, a huge cemetery on the other. London as we have known it quickly transforms into something remote, leafy, industrial. We continue on and on, under Wood Lane and on to Park Royal. The air smells sweet, of sugar, sulphur and oats. It feels good to be getting out.

The Grand Union cuts through the middle of the Park Royal trading estate, which Harry Wallop in the *Telegraph* dubbed 'the breadbasket of the capital'.[104] Heinz and Guinness may have moved out in 2000 and 2004 respectively – there's no longer a whiff of baked beans or beer

– but there are still 489 food companies operating on this 1,800-acre site, employing more than 15,000 people. According to Wallop, McVitie's makes 400 tonnes of biscuits every day in its Park Royal factory. No wonder the air smells so syrup-sweet.

When we're cruising on the Regent's Canal in town I usually do the lock gates. I'm better at exerting brute force on a stiff paddle than I am performing manoeuvres. But I drive now, free from London's traffic, tight patches and terrors. It's wonderfully empty and clear. Flat-sided warehouses present blank faces to the water. Crack willows droop and dip into the Cut. Gliding round bends and under bridges I regain my nerve. I can captain this ship, this boat of ours that is alive with the buzz of the engine. The vibrations pulse through the tiller and into my steering arm. I turn my mind to the logic of the water, remembering to steer not from the front but the back. Push the tiller this way, Pike's nose will move in the other direction; it's easy really.

Driving is generally a series of gentle nudges, a little bit to the right, a little to the left. There are blind bends and floating obstacles to avoid that require more exaggerated steering. Here, low-hanging trees grasp at our bicycles and boat hooks and try to whip them off the roof. I take note of the wind, which is faint but still present, reading the patterns it makes on the water and predicting how the canal-side buildings might alter its course. New builds, with their sheer faces of metal and glass, create tricksy wind traps and tunnels.

By and by, we come to a two-lane aqueduct that passes high over the six-lane North Circular. I align the boat to the right, driving dead slow into the narrow channel and then straight over the road. A small narrowboat overtakes on the left. Let him be fast, we will be slow. Flying by way of water over a jammed gyratory is a joy to savour. It could so easily be us down there. Let's revel in our different fate.

On and on and on we go, the sun hot and the water slack. We eat lunch as we cruise, a holiday picnic of cheese and pickle sandwiches and Mr Kipling's Bramley apple pies. From Alperton on it feels like we're in the country. The river, as we now imagine the Grand Union to be, is bottle green and sky blue, absorbing all the colour overhanging it, reflecting back all of the leaves. Time has loosened right off.

A curious young heron takes an interest in us, flying just ahead but always stopping to look back. Together we approach a herd of Canada geese which, disturbed, are spurred into a fly-by, low over our heads. We see very few boats, but we do see the occasional cyclist and walker on the towpath, and workers from the industrial units taking cigarette breaks. We disturb a man sunbathing on a cardboard box, who darts into the undergrowth like a startled deer. And we see a mallard drake sharing a nest with a coot. We have gone down the rabbit hole and up the magic faraway tree.

Pleased with our progress and fuddled by the unexpected heat, we decide to stop at four o'clock. We slot neatly into a gap at Greenford, close to a road and the Black Horse pub. Let's keep the dream alive and call them 'a lane' and 'an inn'. They once were. A photograph in the Museum of London archive shows this very spot as it was in July 1930. Men laze about on a humpback bridge and swimmers sunbathe on the canal's dreamy banks, the Black Horse on hand for a refreshing ale.[105] Today the country bridge has gone, as have the bathers; industry hums and there's litter in the bushes, but if we close our eyes to these details this place is still close to idyllic.

A walk to the nearest high street comprehensively shatters the illusion. Here are London's red double-decker buses, grinding past three convenience stores, two betting shops, an Irish bar, a funeral director's and the ubiquitous fried chicken shop. We are clearly still within the capital's sprawl. We buy milk, beer and salted nuts and head back to our enclave to lie on the roof until the sun drops. A cormorant balances on the top branch of a tall pine tree: a good omen for the remaining voyage out. It's briefly bothered by a couple of crows, then left in peace to preen on its narrow perch, which bends double under its weight.

We set out again mid-morning, slow-sliding along the top edge of Perivale Wood and through the western corner of Horsenden Hill. We relax into a stroll pace that allows us long looks into the brambly hedgerows, parkland and woods, where the sun picks out the eye-popping details. A dusty peach and pale blue crow, dear old jay bird, flapping between the trees. The fluorescent purple, pink and cyan wisp of a fisherman's fly caught in the grip of a low-hanging branch. An orange sweater, once sodden, now dried stiff, pinned out of shape across a thorny bush. The vermilion of a moorhen's beak, its bright yellow tip. A mallard's electric-blue speculum. The leathery banana cheek of a cormorant as it overtakes us, sewing long, loose running stitches across the water.

We soon reach Bull's Bridge, which marks the end of the Paddington Branch, a T-junction over which an immense 24-hour Tesco looms. A left turn here would take us down to the Thames at Brentford; right is the way to Uxbridge. Between here and the boatyard we cruise first parallel to the M4, then the M25, separated from the roads by a wide barrier of lakes and streams. We pass an aggregates plant that shudders and coughs and fills the air with dust. At Southall a crowd of geese, swans and pigeons swarms around something flung out from the Quality Foods depot; a little further on mallards roost and a swan has a good peck at some geese.

There are missing posters pasted up everywhere. A schoolgirl called Alice has disappeared, last seen walking along the towpath near Brentford. Sun-bleached paper pinned to trees and posts expresses her parents' growing despair and local people's disbelief. The canal's sinister undertones begin to exert themselves and a gloom descends. In the end we turn away from the posters; what else can we do? The girl's body will later be found in the canalised River Brent, the body of her suspected killer in Boston Manor Park.

We pass several residential moorings on our way north, suburbia afloat. Some moorings are well established and have pretty cottage gardens, with sheds, tables and chairs, and lines of washing pegged out. Others are more haphazard. The houseboats range from freshly painted Dutch barges to mouldering prefabs. People are out working in the sun – with a laptop, a grinder, a paintbrush. I add some beauties to my growing boat name collection: Larkspur, Hawkweed, Tiercel, Eva Luna, The Whole of the Moon.

We arrive in south Cowley mid-afternoon and moor up below the lock. As in Greenford, with a little imagination we can just about convince ourselves we're in the country-side despite the surrounding housing estates and industry. It's busier than Greenford but Cowley has more of a village feel, with its lock-keeper's cottage and towing path pub. London feels much further off; here we can cross a bridge into Buckinghamshire. Boats with long-term moorings are strung down the offside bank below the lock; we park up in a visitor mooring opposite. Fish jump, birds sing, planes hum, kids shout, dogs bark, we flake out.

We spend the next morning exploring. On the map the area between the canal and the motorway is more blue than it is green or grey, veined with meandering waterways and large ponds. We walk to Little Britain Lake, which takes its name from its shape and is half-solid with duckweed. More coots than I have ever seen flocked together before are ploughing dark patterns into the matted green surface as they move about.

The Frayes and Colne Rivers run through the woods close by, shallow and narrow, more like streams. Whatever their width and depth, the fast-moving water seems particularly fresh and alive after the flat canal. These rushing streams are reminders that the Cut is manipulated by engine, oar, wind or waterbird; it has no dynamism of its own.

We play a half-hearted game of Poohsticks and later find more pleasure in throwing just-fallen conkers – so deep and dark they look newly varnished – into the river, making music with their plops. Kids jump fully clothed from a footbridge into the water, delighting in a hot, late September day by bunking off. The weather phenomenon has now officially been christened the 'continental blowtorch' by the papers, which has none of the romance of an Indian summer and suggests something angry and short-lived. It's language at odds with the actual weather, which is not, after all, scorching, and with the happiness one feels when the summer goes on and on like this, lulling us into thinking it could be endless.

Due in dry dock at 8.30 the next morning, we head back to the boat and cruise on to Uxbridge, which takes about an hour. We tie up almost opposite the boatyard, close to a yowling dog and nineteen hours early for our appointment. We must be keen, nervous or both. We spend the evening revising our plan for the next seven days, picking over everything that's making us anxious, and suffer a sleepless night.

15. underbelly

The continental blowtorch continues to burn; this September morning could easily be early August. We sit on deck eating breakfast in the sun, watching a large barge manoeuvre out of Uxbridge dry dock. It backs out bottom first, then swings slowly around and slides past us, freshly painted scarlet and heading south. The dry dock is, in essence, a short, covered inlet off the main canal, with a single set of lock gates to either let water in or shut it out. A boat slots in while it's full, the gates are closed behind it, the water is pumped out and the vessel emerges in a dry underground space, where it's possible to work on the hull.

Fed, we prepare to take our turn, untying Pike's ropes, pushing off and gently powering over to the opposite bank. The balmy, peaceful morning belies our growing anxiety about the unknown ahead. We feel our novice status sharply; for me, our ignorance is experienced as a tight squeeze around the belly and a thrumming in the chest.

We approach the yard and are instructed to kill the engine and wait. Two men take over, guiding Pike off the canal and into the covered dock. It's a hangar-like space with a large pool in the middle and a narrow walkway running around the edge. The men pull Pike right to the end of the dock and tie her up; we remain on the boat. They shut the lock gates, cutting the pool off from the canal, and turn on the pump that will suck the water out. S. has been severe all morning but brightens now. We're in and we're safely draining. In celebration, we resolve to have more tea and toast. The men have been almost entirely silent, but we establish it will take about three hours for the pool to fully empty out.

The rush of the morning, the nerves and the anticipation, abruptly stop. A pause. Three hours. A loss of momentum looms. We help each other off the boat and stand on the dockside, watching for the water level to drop. It's barely discernible at first but Pike gradually begins to sink and then a widening ring of green, brown, black appears on the side of the boat as parts of her we don't usually see appear. A shoal of fish swim in circles in the shrinking pool, trapped and desperate. We plan to scoop them out once the water level is lower but never see them again, alive or dead.

Second cup of tea drained from the mug and the dock still looking full, we understand it will not be possible to stand here and watch water drain for three hours straight.

We tentatively explore the boatyard, curious but cautious not to get in the way. It's full of activity and noise this morning, the busiest it will be. Saturday is changeover day, and there are several boats leaving and several arriving, the crane hoisting vessels smaller than ours in and out. Later it will be a much quieter place, with just us living on site. It's a compact complex, with a history that extends back 200 years. The original boatyard was run by canal logistics company Fellows, Moreton & Clayton until 1948. The current owner took it over in the 1970s and today it consists of the covered dry dock and adjacent covered workshop, plus an outside yard and chandlery.[106] A collection of narrowboats sits supported on scaffolds in the workshop and the yard, ungainly in their disrepair.

The chandlery proves the most compelling distraction as we wait for the dock to drain. It's small but well stocked, one of those Tardis-like places that manages to squeeze an extraordinary amount of stuff in. There are polished capstan clocks, coal scuttles, barometers and hurricane lamps, brass dollies and enamelled buckby jugs. There's an entire room of colourful rope and hose, wound up on giant spools. There are heavy cotton smocks, sou'westers, canvas deck shoes and Breton caps for sale, alongside vials of fluid and grease, and a dazzling array of hooks, chains, clasps and bolts, of portholes, fenders, filters and floats. The woman behind the high shop counter proves a friendly fountain of knowledge, and her generous advice eases some of our anxiety about what's expected of us. With her close by, the blacking seems a more manageable job. She guides us through some of our options in terms of bitumen and then leaves us to roam about the shop. The paraphernalia towers, combined with her wise words, have a soothing effect.

We lose hours to the chandlery and return to the dry dock as though from a long trip. Pike has emerged, beached on long wooden struts. For once we can see her entire angular bulk. Without her disguising skirt of water, she is mighty and vulnerable all at once. We climb down into the puddled stone pit to look at her more closely, to run our hands over her bubbled and blistered skin. The newly naked surface presents a scuffed and flocked map of her last six years in the water. A thin stripe of bright green weed marks the waterline, and below that she is matted with soft, tight curls of a darker-coloured plant. There are weeping rust pustules knitted into the curls and they gleam with clinging patches of iridescent oil. Hundreds of blue-black freshwater mussels are clamped to the boat's vast dripping bottom. Their fate has been sealed. I run my hands over them and her, fingering the blisters, then crushing the bubbles flat.

Before we can paint, we have to clean, to pick at Pike's scabs and slough off her distorted skin. Doing it by hand would be an immense job, so we hire a pressure washer and blast her back to her bare bones. The struts only raise the boat 70 centimetres off the ground and the water jet can't completely reach, so I crawl underneath to scrape at the surface with a rigid plastic paddle. It's only just possible to crouch, head cocked awkwardly to one side, cheek against cool rough steel. I crawl through silt puddles and blasted mollusc. It smells of salt, wet stone and death.

Washed and dried, the steel hull resembles an ancient rock, water-worn and camo-printed with smears of dark burgundy, pale yellow and pastel green. Shuffling to her furthest under-reaches, and scuffing my own skin on hers, I begin to feel like I more fully understand Pike's make-up. When we float she is an enigma, but in here I can get to know her shape and girth. By scouring off her dead skin together, S. and I are laying more of a claim, making Pike belong more wholly to us.

It's late now and the yard is empty. We retreat into the boat, climbing down into the dock and up onto her using ladders. It is strange to moor inside, with our home's struc-ture caught up within another one. It makes our domestic world seem miniature, a doll's house. The hangar is harshly lit with strip lights, half dungeon, half shed, with a curved corrugated roof that lets the weather in. Down in the pool it is damp. Water leaks through a gap in the gate, and there's the constant sound of rushing water as a pump works to keep the canal out. The pressure washing and scraping have been exhausting and, despite the strange surroundings and the wall of white noise, we find it easy to sleep.

The next morning we help each other into our hooded all-in-one white dust suits. We put blue plastic shoe covers over our walking boots, clip paper dust masks onto our faces and pull on one-size-doesn't-fit-all blue latex gloves. We lay newspaper across the kitchen floor and on the front deck. And then we begin the blacking, taking one side of the boat each. The bitumen is as thick and dark as molasses, heavy and solvent-smelling. It takes about two hours to paint our respective sides; we start at the bow and meet again at the stern. It's hard work but immediately gratifying. Pike's pockmarked skin is transformed with just one coat. The high-shine paint makes her look brand new.

The bottom of the hull is a huge challenge that we have to tackle next, made worse by the uncomfortably small amount the boat is raised off the ground. Who wants to spend a significant amount of time in a space only 70 centimetres high? S. stoically takes on the middle section, shifting around under the boat flat on his back, balanced on a plank. There's a canvas of 570 square feet to cover. I focus on the under-edges, which I can do on my knees rather than my back. It takes hours. S.'s paintbrush looks fine but mine comes to resemble a hedgehog. Sharp, thin pains shoot up my painting wrist. S. suffers silently under the boat. By the time we finish, we are both wet, miserable and covered in bitumen. We peel off our stained suits and hang them, like animal skins, from the rafters to dry, then use white spirit to remove the tacky spits and spats from our cheeks.

We will do three coats in all, leaving 24 hours drying time between each one. On drying days we do odd jobs on the rest of the boat, patching scrapes and fixing things up. We scurry about low down in our damp cavern and the outside world comes to feel a long way off. The days slip on, we slap on more bitumen, and we wait for it to dry. Each layer is more tedious than the last, and there's no longer that first satisfaction of seeing where we've been. We paint gloss on top of gloss, and we get stickier and messier day by day. Our hands are swollen, our eyes pink from the fumes. The last coat finally on, it needs 48 hours to dry before the boat goes back in the water.

Pike is susceptible to mechanical corrosion caused

by friction – scraping along walls, running aground and bumping about in locks – which is why we protect the hull with a buffer of several layers of bitumen like this. She's also vulnerable to electro-chemical corrosion caused by galvanism, so in our two spare days we attach a couple of new magnesium anodes to the hull. Galvanism is the flow of electrons that occurs when two different metals are brought together in an electrolyte-like water. Although Pike is mainly made from steel, she has a bronze alloy propeller and a brass stern gland. Underwater, a charge will begin to flow between these metals and, because steel is the most reactive of the three, it will begin to wear away. The magnesium anodes are large, sacrificial tablets made from a metal that is more reactive in fresh water than steel. The idea is that these anodes corrode instead of the hull.

The more time we spend in dry dock, and the more time we think about things like galvanism and anodes, the more Pike reminds me of Robert Pirsig's motorcycle; I am starting to think our boat and his bike have something in common. In *Zen and the Art of Motorcycle Maintenance*, Pirsig draws out and explores the distinction between the vehicle itself and what it facilitates. Our relationship with Pike is both classic and romantic, in the *Zen and the Art ...* sense. The romantic sees the bike/boat as a vessel for adventure and for life, the classic sees its underlying form, its component parts and how it works. Although motorcycle riding – or boating – is romantic, the maintenance of the vehicle is purely classic.

Pirsig shows how, while some of us might resist the coupling, the romantic and the classic are ultimately married. By practising the art of motorcycle – or canal boat – maintenance, you learn to appreciate how the classic and the romantic might each inform and enhance the other. The process of blacking the boat, although laborious, is re-shaping our understanding, and therefore enjoyment, of it. Gradually getting to grips with Pike's underlying form is proving as illuminating as it is dirty and difficult.

Seven days have passed, and this morning the silent men will return to refill the dock. The water starts rushing in as promised at 7.30. It's a far faster rewinding than we expect, and Pike is floating again before eight o'clock. We back out of the dock and onto the Grand Union once more, pointing the nose south-east towards town. It's a lovely morning, the sun fragmenting the Cut into a thousand copper and silver shards. We squint at the water and at each other, elated, proud and, most of all, extremely pleased to be out.

16. adrift

South out of the boatyard, then east onto the Paddington Branch and straight on 'til evening. Another night in Greenford and then onwards into town. The journey is a good one. The weather continues to be kind, the canal peaceful and all our own. It's October in a few days but, even now, it still could be August. We move at our snail's pace in just our shirtsleeves. The banks along the way are carpeted with Michaelmas daisies, a cheerful autumn wildflower that likes to lay its roots by static water. Made daft by the unseasonal heat and the endless violet blooms, we make wild plans for further trips, competing to lay out the most complicated routes we could take by water across the UK and Europe. We revel in our mobility, our freedom to go wherever we like. It's ludicrous of course. Despite feeling like we've been to another country, we haven't actually left London once during our short trip. We have been bound inside the M25 at all times.

There is a lightness to our cruising now the blacking is done but also a niggle about where to moor next. We have decided to stay west for a while but who knows where the Pike-shape gaps will be. Journeying without a defined destination – but knowing we need to stop because we are not free from work, from commitments, from a clawing attachment to one specific city – continues to be a challenge. Part of me is excited, the other part feels queasy. There's adrenalin somewhere in this mix. Maybe Mr Lies was telling the truth when he said: 'It's the price of rootlessness. Motion sickness. The only cure: To keep moving.'[107]

Within a few hours we reach Kensal Green and become instantly practical. As we pass the gasworks, a gap opens out opposite the cemetery's south-eastern corner. We confer and agree that yes, this will be our home for the next two weeks. I pull myself up onto the roof and walk to the front to get ready with the front rope. S. swings the stern out and noses the bow close to the bank so I can jump off. We fit in neatly but decide to turn the boat round so the hatch and bedroom window face onto the water instead of the towpath. The canal is wide enough but it's a tricky manoeuvre which brings out our new neighbour, concerned we are going to crash. The bank on the cemetery side is silty and S. has to use the boat pole to punt us through the sticky shallows. A brief flash of fear that we are stuck passes and we swing round, nestling into position with no danger of hitting the neighbour's boat. It's nice to meet him, shake hands, know his name and hear his thoughts on the canal in this particular spot. His boat is a tiny plastic cruiser and Pike is enormous in comparison. We must have cast a terrifying shadow as we turned.

Pins struck into the bank, ropes knotted and weed hatch cleared, we sink into the sofa, head to head, hand in hand, and listen to our new surroundings. Boat engine, one poppier than ours. Crows. Creaking tyres. The metallic crack of mallet on mooring pin. Water lapping. Church bells. A single explosive quack.

We are exhausted in exactly the same way and, post-blacking, there is a new solidarity between us. I know this man more now. We make a good team. I have a growing sense of security that contrasts with everything else, which feels increasingly in flux. Home is unfixed, writing work is hand-to-mouth, once-stable friendships are suddenly fluid. I hit 30 and things shifted, almost overnight. There was the predictable stream of new jobs, new cities, marriages, children: other people's new decade and their own new approach. The social network that allowed me to make sense of London, and of life, changed. Left behind, one has to readjust, to find new friends and people to trust. I keep making mistakes.

A new place then, a new area to understand. We haven't moored here before so I study a map. We are at the top of

Ladbroke Grove. The Grand Union is a border – south of it, and downhill, lies the Portobello Road and, eventually, Notting Hill; to the north, sloping upwards, are Kensal Green and Kensal Rise. Counter's Creek passes under the Cut somewhere along here, the lost waterway that marks the border between the boroughs of Hammersmith and Fulham to the west and Kensington and Chelsea to the east. Over the next few days I will come to learn that Kensal Green has a pub serving a decent roast dinner, and that taking a train from Kensal Rise is the fastest route into Highbury and the north London I know best. I will discover that Ladbroke Grove morphs from down-at-heel to chic in a matter of metres, but that those specific metres are difficult to define. I will be reminded that Portobello Market is a hellish tourist trap and the Hammersmith and City Line a source of endless frustration. Beyond the towpath, I will never feel quite at home here; for the next two weeks belonging will remain just out of reach.

The canal seems to get more beautiful the more time I spend on it, a beauty that in this instance comes primarily from its proximity to Kensal Green Cemetery. The graveyard's mature crack willow, ash and sycamore line up along the water's edge. Still with their leaves despite the season, they canopy over the canal in a blur of browns and greens. The trees have an under-storey of hawthorn, elder and privet, and a ground flora of bramble and ivy. The view from our water-facing windows offers a doubling of this – an intense picture of the trees and shrubs and of their glassy reflections. Clouds and leaves and bush and briar, above and below. The towpath in this spot is the widest I think I've ever seen it in London, with a lawn verge that runs right down to the water. The gasworks on the towpath side are kept separate by a brightly inked, high red-brick wall. The path is used but comparatively quiet, nowhere near as hectic as in central London and the east. It isn't lit and for once we aren't overlooked. There are cormorants, herons, geese and ducks by day, and dancing bats at dusk.

It's peaceful, but it won't last. The surrounding area to the west, north and south of the canal is soon to be developed as Old Oak Common; there will be a football stadium, a station and tens of thousands of new homes. BBC News has called it 'one of the largest regeneration schemes in London for decades'.[108] Here's hoping it will be sensitive to the spirit of the place, that the housing will be affordable and the Cut's personality kept.

A kink in the canal here shields us from a huge waterside Sainsbury's, complete with its own 'stop and shop' moorings. It's ugly but, as well as being useful for supplies, the supermarket does a good thing in attracting people onto the towpath and, naturally, they come bearing gifts. The railings outside are permanently lined with sandwich-fancying pigeons, black-headed gulls and geese.

Autumn, which has been stalling for so long, arrives at last. It was in the air last night as a faint whiff of woodsmoke, and it was there this morning in the cold sweat of condensation on the windows inside. It was in the dew balling on the long grass and slicking over Pike's steel shell. And on my walk to the station, it was caught in the cemetery trees that are now burnished with a richer kind of light. The leaves sighed to yellow, crisped up, before my very eyes. This evening the sun glooped below the buildings in an eggy pool, in a way it never would in summer. Tonight we will have our first fire for over six months. The cabin will once more be thick with a soporific dry heat that swallows you up. I can't wait. I walk home along the dark towpath, hugging down deep into my jacket and holding a bike light before me so I can be seen, thinking this is the golden month, the delicious die back and cooling off, before the real cold sets in.

Paradise, as G.K. Chesterton informs us, lies by way of Kensal Green.[109] I want to get to know the cemetery, so I invite S. to join me on a walk with the promise of seeing someone famous's grave. Our list includes Harold Pinter,

Terence Rattigan, Wilkie Collins, Anthony Trollope and the Brunels. The Grand Union runs along the cemetery's southern limit, the Harrow Road along its top, with 72 acres of grey and green in between. The canal was once an integral part of operations: coffins and mourners would arrive by boat, dropped off at a specially built jetty. The original design for Kensal Green – which is the largest of London's 'Magnificent Seven' cemeteries and was the first to open – included an elaborate canal gate, though it was sadly never built.

As well as row upon row of gravestones, Kensal Green has august family tombs, busts and monuments, and large, fridge-cold catacombs below its two chapels. The stone, marble and lawn are laid out formally among tall trees and high hedgerows, attracting songbirds and squirrels. The cemetery is designated a Site of Importance for Nature Conservation, no doubt due to its waterside fringes where the flora is particularly knotty and dense. Crows hop, robins flit, blackbirds sing, parakeets screech. Old headstones are lichen-printed; old graves creep with sedums and moss. Aside from the screams of parrots, the older parts of the cemetery are quiet, calm and classical, crumbling into a perfectly romantic, ivy-laced collapse.

Despite initially giving the impression of a relic, the cemetery is still operational and bodies are interned and ashes regularly spread. New graves are sporadically inter-spersed with the old but are concentrated at the western end. While the Victorian graves are faded and mostly for-gotten, the tightly packed new ones are vivid with fresh grief. Highly polished marble and gold-leaf headstones are adorned with dazzling offerings to the recently dead: acid-bright fake flowers, cartoonish garden ornaments, shiny foil windmills, weather-beaten teddies and toys. Overwhelmed, we retreat back towards the older, more sober eastern part of the cemetery. A kind man in a car pulls up beside us to warn we are about to get locked in, although his concern doesn't extend to a lift. The closest gate is already locked so we have to double back again to the westerly exit.

Free of the graveyard, it's a long tramp down Harrow Road and over Ladbroke Grove back to the boat, and as we tramp we lament that we found none of the famous graves we were supposed to. It was an impossible task without a guide or a map. What we did see, however, was an enormous pile of wood, the result of regular clearing and coppicing. Some of the logs looked seasoned, as if they might have been there for a year or more. S. is excited and calls the cemetery the next day to ask what is planned for the wood pile. They explain it is due to be removed any day now and yes, in the meantime, we can help ourselves.

It's a brilliant bit of luck. Wood isn't easy to get hold of in town and buying it is expensive and troublesome without a delivery address. So S. sets about bringing it back, bit by bit, in the bike trailer, making several trips over the course of an afternoon. His instinct to stockpile for winter is becoming strong again. He stacks the logs carefully in boxes on the roof and in the engine room, selecting the most attractive pieces to dry out by the stove. He does all this while I'm out on a job, and it's a surprise to come home to. I'm pleased and grateful but disgruntled too; his torn skin and splinters make me feel guilty.

Establishing a first home with a partner is a fraught process. I had never lived alone with just a boyfriend before buying the boat, and getting the division of labour right can be difficult. Although we both consciously resist, tasks have an annoying tendency to fall along gender lines. S. greases the stern gland, I clean the loo. I garden, he collects and stores firewood. I find myself giving in to his superior ability to tie a secure knot, encouraging him to tie them all rather than improving at knotting myself. In turn, I worry about pulling my weight and compensate by cleaning.

This is the first time I have ever been drawn to housework, as both a bribe and a solace. There's part of me that has resisted domesticity as a way of staying young, free and reckless – which I know is embarrassing and makes me ridiculous as well as slovenly – and there's another part of me that is now finding comfort in keeping house. My previous self and the new one are still negotiating. Everyday chores on the canal are distinct from those on land, I tell myself, horrified to suddenly be finding satisfaction in the washing up. Domesticity is hard-won on a boat and so it's more acceptable to enjoy it. This hot water took a lot of physical effort – we drove the boat to a towpath water point, filled the tank by hose and by hand, chopped the wood and heaved the coal, then built the fire that warmed it up. On Pike, washing up water isn't just on tap.

Perhaps my discomfort with the domestic is feeding a desire to focus on things outside of the boat, to turn my attention away from myself. Our recent trip to Uxbridge made me think more about the wider canal system and how it works. It reminded me how the canal sits always waiting, be it for boat or fowl; that it's a body of water that doesn't well up from the earth or gouge out its own route to the sea. If there's no spring, where does the water come from? Beyond rain and run-off, what are its water roots?

I journey north-west out to Hendon on the tube in search of sources. The plan is to visit Welsh Harp Reservoir and then follow a thin feeder channel from there back to the Grand Union near Harlesden. There should be an outlet where the feeder meets the Cut two and half miles west of where we're currently moored. What am I hoping for? A greater understanding of what Pike's floating upon and a simple excursion I guess. I want to walk unfamiliar streets, to satisfy a weird craving I have for the downbeat suburbia that exists beyond the city's core. Seeing more of modern-day Metroland suits my mood.

The Welsh Harp Reservoir – named after a local hostelry that was once infamous – was conceived as early as 1803 but not finished until 1837. The hay meadow valleys of the River Brent and the Silk Stream were dammed and flooded to create an additional water supply for the canal network, alongside existing reservoirs at Ruislip and Aldenham. Along with leakage and evaporation, 250 cubic metres is lost from the high level of the canal to the low level every time a boat passes through a lock. If the canal isn't restocked, water levels could drop to unnavigable depths.

R.S.R. Fitter points out in *London's Natural History* that the reservoir has long served wildlife as well as the canals, reporting that 'in the mid-19th century it became one of the most famous localities in the country for rare wildfowl'. Birds recorded in 1866 included squacco heron, night heron, little bittern, ferruginous duck, avocet and grey phalarope. Today, things are a lot less rural but the site is protected as a Site of Special Scientific Interest and part of the land surrounding the water is managed as a nature reserve.

Despite its size, for the uninitiated Welsh Harp is hard to find when approaching from Hendon Central on foot. There's a miserable nub of water on West Hendon Broadway, lurking in the shadow of a superstore, and then I see no sign of it for twenty minutes or more as I traipse over gull-dotted but otherwise empty playing fields in pursuit. The ground slopes upwards, becoming increasingly muddy underfoot. There's a vigorous clump of gorse on the summit but no sweeping view across a lake. I reach a road but still no reservoir, though by now a dog walker has assured me that it is definitely this way. My first glimpse comes a few minutes later in a gap between trees. It is a dark slab in the distance, inert and fenced off at the feet of another sloping sports field. I carry on down the lane.

When I finally reach Welsh Harp Open Space, with its old oaks, briars and bracken, I feel relieved. After the train and trudging about, I'm here at last, at the canal's beginning. The reservoir edge is within reach and the usual suspects – swans, coots, black-headed gulls, mallards, Canada geese – dabble close to the bank. The water glisters and rolls, ribbed by the breeze and the ducks. Three yellow roses on long stems float just below the surface, in memoriam, or a rejected bouquet. This would be a good spot to pay one's respects – and for an argument. Across the reservoir there is a busy road and row upon row of houses, and the water itself is dotted with giant orange buoys to mark out lanes for water sports, but, alone in the long grass, I can see that there is a wildness here too. A root-ruptured path winds through the bronze and buff undergrowth, away from the water and into the nature reserve, past trees encrusted with gold lichen and blackberry bushes with branches that hoop over in just the same way the Wembley Arch does in the distance.

It's a small reserve and, after a brief wander, I find myself in a car park all too soon, one where signboards tell me about all the creatures I might have seen in the grassland, marsh and woods if only I'd looked. Masts from the nearby sailing club tinkle rapidly in the wind. The only other person here is a man in a UPS van, fast asleep, his head on the steering wheel, his arms laced through it as though in an embrace. There's a concrete dam and weir at the reservoir's southern edge, a reminder of its origins and its purpose, and of why I'm here. It's a militaristic structure, with a khaki green cabin on top. It's from this point that the feeder sets out on its course through Metroland to the canal. Visible only in snatches, it passes through residential streets and around lonely recreation grounds, puddles up in the wake of depots and retail parks, and tunnels beneath busy roads and wide railway tracks.

It's possible to follow the feeder for some of its journey south through Neasden and Stonebridge Park, although tracking its course often feels like an illicit pursuit. After leaving the Welsh Harp, it immediately disappears behind a cluster of houses and shops before emerging from under the A4088 along the eastern edge of a deserted recreation ground. It runs between this and a row of back gardens, its narrow banks grassy and littered. A large pipe forms a bridge over the shallow channel, which is about a metre and a half wide, and allows me to cross the water and then walk for about 50 metres alongside it, scaring reclusive moorhens who thought they'd found somewhere safe to hide. I urge myself onwards, only partly shaking off a feeling that I'm a trespasser and soon to be told off. The bank becomes increasingly overgrown and eventually impassable. The feeder slips out of reach and I have to turn back.

I find it again after walking east then south along the North Circular Road – an alarming experience, like walking headlong into a violent gale but with none of the romance and, it seems, all of London's lorries in howling attendance. The feeder reappears, behind bars now, trapped between a giant Ikea and a giant Tesco. A plastic bag flaps lamely in the water, a sad sort of jellyfish. The feeder flees this miserable scene by tunnelling under six lanes of traffic and out into the open on the other side, where it runs behind a row of terraced houses. I trace its course down parallel Woodheyes Road and glimpse it again at the end of the street, now running alongside Bridge Road Allotments but padlocked out of reach.

The map describes a 90-degree turn the feeder will make and suggests I will be able to meet it again running along the edge of Gibbons Recreation Ground. This part of Zone 4 is rich in close-cropped recs. I head there, where I can indeed walk along the channel's grassy banks once more. This time there is a line of coppiced trees down one side, their stout trunks topped with mohawks of thin branches, and views of Neasden Temple's chalky-white domes in the distance. The narrow waterway does have some charm – and local people are awake to its potential as a water feature, organising occasional clean-ups and litter picks – but it would take a large leap of imagination to recast the feeder from murky ditch into babbling brook.

After a few minutes walking along the water my way is blocked again and I have to squeeze out through a gap in the fence, which already gapes from previous visitors. Back on the street, I decide to take a more direct route south, then west to meet the feeder as it runs through yet another rec, this time by a road called Hillside. When I find it there it is like a formal park feature, albeit an unloved one, cutting through some short grass that is predictably used as a place for dogs to defecate. The feeder tunnels away under another road, reappearing prettily but briefly on the other side before disappearing beneath a mess of train tracks.

I head straight to the canal now, unable to tunnel with the feeder under the railway, instead walking down residential streets named after Shakespeare, Milton and Johnson, past Harlesden station and over two road bridges. There is a strong smell of toasted cheese; today the McVitie's factory must be making Mini Cheddars. I meet the feeder for the final time at its outlet just west of the Grand Junction pub. The spot is unremarkable, distinctive only for a brief widening out of the canal and the gathering flotsam of cans and crisp packets, presumably pulled in by the indiscernible swirl of two water courses meeting. The feeder arrives silent through a square brick opening, greeted by chattering gulls and, today, by me. Although my expectations of the mouth were low, I'm disappointed. I was hoping for more of a rush.

My curiosity extinguished and my feet throbbing as though they might burst my boots, I head east. The walk home is along secluded industrial towpath. I barely see a soul or a boat again until I reach Wormwood Scrubs. The landscape alternates between stripped back and over-grown. Here is metal, concrete, gravel, razor wire, distant cranes in the sky. Here too is soft earth, bramble tangle, mushroom and moss. In places the trees bow over on both sides of the water to almost meet in the middle, creating a tunnel-like, holloway effect. Despite the solitariness, there is always brightly spray-painted brick to remind me that I'm not the first, that people have been here before and performed acrobatic feats to splash this green-grey-brown place with pink, red and white.

Buddleia, bramble and ivy abound, also hazel, haw-thorn and crimson-stemmed dogwood. There's a tiny oak tree, struggling it seems, and then three silver birches in close conversation. Branched bur-reed and sedges soften the water edge at points. There's a mouldering mattress. A sodden cuddly toy. A trainer in a tree. Every bridge has its obligatory rubbish pile, the gathering plastic detritus that will outlive us all. Most of the canal-side buildings are modern warehouse units, large blank blue-grey cuboids that have no obvious interaction with the Cut. An older, attractive brick warehouse presents a friendlier face to the water. It might once have had an intimate relationship with the Grand Union, with materials and fuel arriving, and goods leaving, by barge rather than road. Fourteen gulls stand single file on the peak of its sloping tile roof, beaks all pointing north.

Onwards and small residential moorings start to spring up. Shipping containers stacked by the waterside are converted into workplaces, grassy slopes have the occasional barbecue and bench. This evening there is nobody about, but people have left their traces. Some nights the Cut here must buzz. Past the Scrubs, which is out there but not seen, the Kensal Green gasometers come into view, their redundant wrought iron encircling fat cakes of thin air. The towpath falls in close step with the rail tracks on the approach into town. It's dusky, getting dark, cool and damp. The weather takes a turn for the worse.

I start thinking about Michael Moorcock's 1988 novel about the capital, *Mother London*. In it, the author describes this part of North Kensington as it was between 1940 and 1985 in cacophonous detail. In one decade London is terrifyingly laid waste by airborne bombers; 40 years later it is slowly being re-formed by developers and the 'bland standardising merchants' that sheepishly follow them in. As I plough on through the thickening gloom towards the boat, hungry and wet, I imagine Moorcock's characters Beth and Chloe Scaramanga taking tea somewhere in the bleak beyond, and the clairvoyant Josef Kiss and his demons stumbling along this very towpath to find them. Out there amid a chaos of cable and train track, the foundations of their home, Bank Cottage, lie crumbling into dust.

I have fallen in love with Beth and Chloe, and the life they have carved out for themselves. The sisters raise fancy chickens in their cottage garden and board other people's pets, living an 'astonishingly rural' existence under the protection of the coke-carrying barge folk, as their beloved city throbs and growls around them. Unconventional as they are, Beth and Chloe are a source of stability throughout the book. For me, their canal-side cottage with its high yew hedges, its private mooring and skiff, its 'stone and timber and thatch', comes to represent a sense of liberty, despite the physical digging in. There is also a comforting familiarity in Bank Cottage's pewter and copper, its old fashioned fire, trivet and stovetop kettle, the murmur of traffic on a distant canal bridge filtering through the windows, the biscuit tin where Harlequin and Columbine dance. It sounds just like home.

Moorcock shows how the canal-scape changes over the decades. Although London, for his character Josef Kiss, is losing her soul – isn't she always? – the Grand Union does transform for the better over the 45 years the novel inhabits. When Josef first crashes along the towpath in the midst of the Blitz, it is still private land. Later, his friend and lover, Mrs Gasalee, recalls a visit to the Scaramanga sisters not long after the war. The towpath and waterway are grotty and uncared for. She arrives at Bank Cottage 'with her shoes caked in yellow mud and had more than once on the way been afraid she would fall into the filthy water and be poisoned'.

We find the lovers strolling along the towpath again in the 1980s, when the network has been nationalised for three decades and the revival is beginning to take hold. The canal is a completely different place: 'Now men and boys fished there and occasionally an elaborately painted barge went past like a scene from *The Water Gypsies*'. If the couple were to walk here today, they would surely comment on how much it has changed again, marvelling at the number of boats moored up along the bank and the people living aboard.

I try to work out exactly where Bank Cottage might have stood, but the walls here are so high it's impossible to get a grip on the lay of the land. I wonder if the winding hole close to the supermarket, where there is space for a canal boat to turn, might have been where the women kept their small boat but, no, it is too close to Ladbroke Grove. All I know for sure is the cottage was overshadowed by the gasworks and had views of the cemetery, just as we do from Pike right now. The difference is that the Scaramangas remained in their one spot for years on end, static enough to become knitted into the fabric of the city. For their friends, Beth and Chloe and Bank Cottage are as one; the stone and timber and thatch as much a part of them as their ageing bones and flesh. The sisters will never leave, except when death takes them. I envy them their attachment to one place, the way they can make their surroundings truly their own. I read and reread the chapters about them while we are moored here, hoping to infect myself with their easy sense of being where they belong.

Out of nowhere – perhaps willed into existence by my repetitive reading – the possibility of a more long-term mooring for Pike arises, a pitch further east on the Regent's Canal. Months ago we put ourselves on a waiting list, then forgot all about it. Far from reacting with a clear *let's do it*, we sink into a mire of pros and cons. The chance to stay put for a few months, maybe years, is compelling, especially as the cold weather sets in. But, despite my *Mother London* reveries, when an ending presents itself I realise that I have become thoroughly used to being unattached.

We visit the residential mooring spot and the overwhelming feelings are fear and grief. How strange. My heart screams *don't do it*, my head reasons that we should at least give it a try, that circumstances right now would make it a good decision, that not having to worry about things like the water running out will surely make work pressures easier to bear. I attempt to get used to the idea by writing my name out with an address, like some soppy teenager trying out a crush's surname. It now looks weird with a fixed abode beneath it.

The question of the long-term mooring is something that will bother us for the rest of the year, a pushing and pulling pit of *will we, won't we, should we, shouldn't we.* Money is a concern: we don't have much and the mooring, though run by a housing association and we think fairly priced, would still be a significant expense. But more than that, to anchor in one place long-term would be to give up by rooting down. Our recent struggles have defined us. A permanent mooring would mean turning our backs on something that has, so far, given us as much pleasure as it has pain.

Journeying together has redefined our relationship, it has made it better, stronger, kinder, more entwined. It has changed our relationship with London too. In this last year alone, we've had the rare privilege of living in at least ten different boroughs. She is a seamier city when experienced from a boat, and a more sublime one. Her contradictions seem starker. But, a fixed place to lash our ropes would allow us to really get to know a specific part of London again, to have that sense of community and connection that comes from not constantly moving on. We'd feel less exposed. Voting in the next election might be easier. There would be a water tap and mains electricity, luxuries not to be dismissed. Boat life would remain rustic, hard even, just easier than before. It's a difficult decision, one we put off by focusing on more pressing concerns.

Two weeks have quickly passed and, more important than making decisions about where we will be in the future, we need to think about where we will be next, today. We will continue eastwards, on towards town. The ritual begins all over again. Engine on. Wooden handle slotted onto steel tiller, brass pin fixing it in place. S. at the stern, tar-black coffee once again steaming from green and brown cup. Me at the bow. *Ready?* Ropes off, pins out, push off, jump on. Sliding forwards, three-and-a-half knots. Round the corner and under the grove. On past tumble-down terraces, sixties tower blocks and curving concrete motion sculptures. Past tufted ducks and Canada geese. Past mallards, moorhens and coots. Under an iron bridge painted red and gold. Adrift, until a Pike-sized gap appears and we stop.

Endnotes

1   L.T.C. Rolt, *Narrowboat*, The History Press, 2013. First published 1944.

2   Richard Mabey, *A Good Parcel of English Soil*, Penguin, 2013.

3   Theo Thomas, 'River of Death, why fish died in the River Lea, and what can be done', Thames 21 website, 27 July 2013.
    http://www.thames21.org.uk/2013/07/river-of-death-why-fish
    -died-in-the-river-lea-and-what-can-be-done/

4   Lee Valley Regional Park Authority, 'Site Management Plan, 2012–17, Walthamstow Marshes'.
    https://www.visitleevalley.org.uk/media/viewfile.ashx?filetype
    =4&filepath=/Nature%20reserves%20and%20open%20spaces/
    Walthamstow%20Marsh%20-%20Site%20Management%20
    Plan%202012-2017.pdf

5   Michael Knowles, *Saving the Walthamstow Marshes*, self-published, 2015.

6   Save the Marshes Campaign, 'Walthamstow Marshes: The 1970s Survey', 2007.
    http://lnhs.org.uk/Images/WalthamstowMarshesSurvey.pdf

7   Emma Bartholomew, 'Protesters haven't given up the fight against Leyton Marsh Olympic basketball hall', *Hackney Gazette*, 5 March 2012.
    http://www.hackneygazette.co.uk/news/heritage/protesters_
    haven_t_given_up_the_fight_against_leyton_marsh_olympic_
    basketball_hall_1_1228437

8   Matthew Beard, 'Hackney Marshes, home of Sunday football, to be bulldozed for Olympics coach park', *Independent*, 1 January 2005.
    http://www.independent.co.uk/sport/olympics/hackney
    -marshes-home-of-sunday-football-to-be-bulldozed-for-olympics
    -coach-park-26702.html

9 Iain Sinclair, *London Orbital*, Penguin, 2003.

10 Mark Cocker and Richard Mabey, *Birds Britannica*, Chatto & Windus, 2005.

11 ibid.

12 'Where are London's starling spectaculars?' RSPB website, 18 November 2010.
http://www.rspb.org.uk/news/details.aspx?id=264649

13 Cocker and Mabey, *Birds Britannica*.

14 Department for Environment, Food and Rural Affairs and Dan Rogerson, 'Celebrating the Canal & River Trust's Olympic Legacy', 3 September 2014.
https://www.gov.uk/government/news/celebrating-the-canal-river-trusts-olympic-legacy

15 Pigment print in the Museum of London archive available to view online at:
http://collections.museumoflondon.org.uk/Online/object.aspx?objectID=object-776232&start=40&rows=1

16 Robert Macfarlane, 'London Fields', *Guardian*, 8 December 2007.
http://www.theguardian.com/books/2007/dec/08/photography

17 Leo Hickman, 'Journey along the river Lee', *Guardian*, 9 October 2009.
http://www.theguardian.com/environment/2009/oct/09/river-lee-polluted-source

18 'Boaters preview Queen Elizabeth Park's waterways', Queen Elizabeth Park website, 6 May 2014.
http://queenelizabetholympicpark.co.uk/news/news-articles/2014/5/queen-elizabeth-olympic-park-opens-its-waterways

19 David Tushingham, 'I already have a golem, many of them. Interview with Paul Barritt', programme for *Golem* by 1927/Young Vic, 2014.

20 Charles Williams, 'Olympic hurdle', *Property Week*, 5 December 2003.
http://www.propertyweek.com/olympic-hurdle/3030828.article

21 Dominik Lemanski, 'Olympic Park affordable housing could be less than a third of promised 50 per cent target', *Hackney Gazette*, 13 October 2014.

http://www.hackneygazette.co.uk/news/olympic_park_
affordable_housing_could_be_less_than_a_third_of_promised_
50_per_cent_target_1_3804842

22   The European Water Framework Directive (WFD) – a European Union (EU) directive established in 2000 – commits EU member states to protect and restore aquatic ecosystems as a basis for ensuring the long-term sustainable use of water for people, business and nature. The Directive's aim of 'good status' for all water bodies by 2015 will not be achieved for a significant proportion of water bodies. At the time of writing, a WFD inspection had not been carried out on Three Mills Lock.
http://eur-lex.europa.eu/legal-content/EN/TXT/PDF/?uri=
CELEX:52012DC0670&from=EN

23   Hickman, 'Journey along the river Lee'.

24   Jonathan Liew, 'London 2012: Barges high and dry as problems hit flow of materials to Olympic Park', *Telegraph*, 12 April 2010.
http://www.telegraph.co.uk/sport/olympics/london-2012/
7583644/London-2012-Barges-high-and-dry-as-problems-hit-flow
-of-materials-to-Olympic-Park.html

'The White Elephant', *Narrowboat World*, 16 April 2010.
http://www.narrowboatworld.com/index.php/
news-flash/1726-what-a-waste

25   'Case Study, Olympic Park, London', Aggregates Industries.
http://www.aggregate.com/documents/case%20studies/
olympic%20park,%20london.pdf

26   'London 2012: From Vision to Reality', Commission for a Sustainable London 2012, November 2012.
http://www.cslondon.org/wp-content/uploads/downloads/
2012/11/CSL_Post%20Games%20Report_Final.pdf

27   Film footage of the Olympic Torch arriving at the Olympic Park in a speedboat captained by David Beckham available to view online at:
https://m.youtube.com/watch?v=Tv27XUiw9NE

28   For example, Colin Saunder's *London, The Definitive Walking Guide* (Cicerone, 2002), p. 137–8 describes: 'Fascinating, easy walking beside backwaters of the River Lea. These adjacent routes in the Lower Lea Project's *Waterways Discovery* series can be walked separately or together ... The longer *Heron Walk* follows the Three

Mills and City Mill rivers, returning by the Old River Lea and Lee Navigation ... and sneaking a peek at Pudding Mill river.'

29   DEFRA and Rogerson, 'Celebrating the Canal & River Trust's Olympic Legacy'.

30   Joanna Taylor, 'Olympic bid demands sale of 3 Mills Studios', *The Stage*, 17 February 2004.
   https://www.thestage.co.uk/news/2004/olympic-bid-demands
   -sale-of-3-mills-studios/

31   When Ikea's property division started its operations in the UK it was known as 'LandProp'. It was rebranded in 2014 and is now called 'Vastint'.
   http://vastint.eu/uk/about-us/

32   Paul Brickell, 'Regeneration Programme – Bromley by Bow', London Legacy Development Corporation, 12 June 2013.
   http://queenelizabetholympicpark.co.uk/~/media/LLDC/
   Committee%20minutes/Committees/Regeneration%20
   and%20Communities%20Committee/12%20June%202013/
   Report4BromleybyBowupdateincludingappendices.pdf

33   http://www.strandeast.com

34   Richard Thomas, 'Bow Locks'.
   http://www.leeandstort.co.uk/Bow_Locks.htm

35   David Fathers, *The Regent's Canal*, Frances Lincoln, 2012.

36   Meg Game and John Whitfield, 'Nature Conservation in Tower Hamlets. Ecology Handbook 27', London Ecology Unit, 1996.

37   Fathers, *The Regent's Canal*.

38   Ted Hughes, 'The Moorhen', *Three Books*, Faber and Faber, 1993.

39   'Standing Water Habitat Action Plan', London Biodiversity Partnership, 2008.
   http://www.lbp.org.uk/downloads/Publications/HabitatInfo/
   SWHAP-FINAL-17-03-08.pdf

40   John Hall, 'Severed head recovered from Regent's Canal where decapitated remains of former EastEnders actress Gemma McCluskie were found', *Independent*, 10 September 2010.
   http://www.independent.co.uk/news/uk/crime/severed-head
   -recovered-from-regents-canal-where-decapitated-remains-of
   -former-eastenders-actress-gemma-mccluskie-were-found-8120976
   .html

Endnotes

41 Louise Gray, 'More than 3,000 shopping trolleys dumped in rivers every year', *Telegraph*, 23 February 2009.
http://www.telegraph.co.uk/news/4788011/More-than-3000
-shopping-trolleys-dumped-in-rivers-every-year.html

42 Cocker and Mabey, *Birds Britannica*.

43 Doris Lessing, *The Golden Notebook*, Fourth Estate, 2013.

44 'The juvenile wagtail, which had scarcely moved a feather whilst it was being fed, suddenly seemed to collapse. Its legs buckled and it sank awkwardly ... Its head arched slowly and cork-screwed round until it was almost facing backwards.' – Richard Mabey, *The Unofficial Countryside*, Little Toller Books, 2010. First published 1973.

45 Emma Gunn, 'How to forage and cook Alexanders', Eden Project website.
http://www.edenproject.com/blog/index.php/2013/05/edible
-wild-food-alexanders/

46 Christopher Grey-Wilson, *Eyewitness Handbooks Wild Flowers of Britain and Northwest Europe*, Dorling Kindersley, 1995.

47 M. Grieve, 'Dropwort, Hemlock Water', *A Modern Herbal*.
https://www.botanical.com/botanical/mgmh/d/drophe21
.html

48 'Control of Hemlock Water Dropwort with Roundup Pro Biactive', Monsanto website.
http://monsanto-live.dbt.co.uk/roundup/roundup-amenity/
aquatic-use/hemlock-water-dropwort/

49 Rachel Carson's book *Silent Spring* was first published in 1962. It exposed the destruction of wildlife through the widespread use of pesticides, and has had a profound impact on the modern eco-logical movement.

50 'Leonardo da Vinci's Canal Lock', Leonardo da Vinci's Inventions website.
http://www.leonardodavincisinventions.com/civil-engineering
-inventions/leonardo-da-vincis-canal-lock/

51 In 2014, there were water points for continuous cruisers on the Regent's Canal at St Pancras Cruising Club, Angel, Victoria Park and Mile End; and black waste disposal at St Pancras and Victoria Park.

52   Alan Wildman as quoted in 'Shapps urges councils to increase houseboat moorings', *BBC News*, 27 August 2007.
http://www.bbc.co.uk/news/uk-14690157

53   Cocker and Mabey, *Birds Britannica.*

54   Fathers, *The Regent's Canal.*

55   'New initiatives launched to help manage London's moorings', Canal and River Trust website, 8 August 2014.
https://canalrivertrust.org.uk/news-and-views/news/
new-initiatives-launched-to-help-manage-londons-moorings

56   London Assembly Environment Committee, 'Moor or less: Mooring on London's Waterways', Greater London Authority, November 2013.
http://www.london.gov.uk/sites/default/files/Moorings%20
report%20agreement%20draft%20FINAL.pdf

57   'New initiatives launched to help manage London's moorings', Canal and River Trust website.

58   London Assembly Environment Committee, 'Moor or less: Mooring on London's Waterways'.

59   Permanent exhibition, London Canal Museum.
http://www.canalmuseum.org.uk
James Meikle and Phil Maynard, 'Canal boats: the last option for affordable city-centre living?' *Guardian*, 11 November 2014.
http://www.theguardian.com/society/2014/nov/11/canal-boat
-affordable-city-centre-living

60   See Lois Pryce, 'Floating voters: How living on a houseboat meant I didn't officially "exist"', *Independent*, 29 March 2015, for more information about the voting situation for boaters.
http://www.independent.co.uk/news/uk/politics/general
election/floating-voters-how-living-on-a-houseboat-meant-i-didnt
-officially-exist-10142337.html

61   'Local councillor Paul Convery accuses boaters apparently wanting "a zone-one location to live, work and play" of opting to live on boats instead of finding housing in lower-cost locations. "Boaters use public services provided by councils but do not pay [council] taxes towards those services. A few send their kids to Islington schools claiming they live in the borough and a few dozen have even registered to vote," he said.' – James Meikle and Phil Maynard, 'Canal boats: the last option for affordable city-centre living?'

62   Rowan Moore, 'Britain's housing crisis is a human disaster. Here are 10 ways to solve it', *Observer*, 15 March 2015.
http://www.theguardian.com/society/2015/mar/14/britain-housing-crisis-10-ways-solve-rowan-moore-general-election

63   'In 2007 the Labour government set a target for 240,000 homes to be built a year by 2016 ... That target has been consistently missed – the closest the UK got was in 2006–07 when 219,000 homes were built. In 2012–13, the UK hit a post-war low of 135,500 homes, much of which was due to the financial crisis. Last year the figure recovered slightly to 141,000 homes. Labour's 2007 target has been dropped by the coalition. In May 2014, Mark Carney, governor of the Bank of England, complained that housebuilding in the UK was half that of his native Canada, despite the UK having a population twice the size. The consequences have been rocketing prices in London, the South East and some other parts of the country.' – Tom de Castella, 'Why can't the UK build 240,000 houses a year?' *BBC News Magazine*, 13 January 2015.
http://www.bbc.co.uk/news/magazine-30776306

64   Daniel Douglas, 'Over 50,000 families shipped out of London boroughs in the past three years due to welfare cuts and soaring rents', *Independent*, 30 April 2015.
http://www.independent.co.uk/news/uk/home-news/over-50000-families-shipped-out-of-london-in-the-past-three-years-due-to-welfare-cuts-and-soaring-10213854.html

65   'It is wrong that having a home in many rural areas, or in London, should be regarded as a luxury. This applies even to traditionally poor London boroughs. "If you can't afford to live in Newham," the borough's mayor told the Focus E15 mothers, "you can't afford to live in Newham." But these people hadn't asked for their neighbourhood to become a high-performing investment asset, and they gain nothing from the change.' – Rowan Moore, 'Britain's housing crisis is a human disaster. Here are 10 ways to solve it'.

66   Canal and River Trust Chief Executive, Richard Parry as quoted in 'Continuous cruisers comply—or you are off!' *Narrowboat World*, 13 February 2015.
http://www.narrowboatworld.com/index.php/news-flash/7738-complyor-you-are-off

67   British Waterways Act, Section 17 available to view online at: http://www.legislation.gov.uk/ukla/1995/1/section/17/enacted

68   'The right to use and live on your boat on waterways owned or managed by the Canal & River Trust (formerly British Waterways) without a permanent mooring is enshrined in Section 17(3)(c)(ii) of the 1995 British Waterways Act. This entitles boat licence holders to stay for up to 14 continuous days in any one place, or longer if the circumstances warrant it. It does not stipulate any specific cruising pattern, minimum distance or "no return within" period beyond this. It does not require boats to be on a "progressive journey". It merely requires boats to be used "bona fide" for navigation ... The standard boat licence entitles boaters to travel where they choose on CRT waterways. There is no legal mechanism whereby CRT can limit the number of boats that navigate in a particular area.' – http://kanda.boatingcommunity.org.uk/about/

69   'Policy outlined for boaters without a home mooring', Canal and River Trust website, 13 February 2015.
    https://canalrivertrust.org.uk/news-and-views/news/policy-outlined-for-boaters-without-a-home-mooring

70   The auction of a Canal and River Trust mooring at Fife Terrace in King's Cross that ended on 3 March 2015 saw bidding push the rent up to £20,015 per annum; the guide price was £6,776.
    https://www.crtmoorings.com/auctions/full_auction_history.php?vacancy_id=7187

71   Peter Ackroyd, *London Under*, Chatto & Windus, 2011.

72   Eric de Maré, *The Canals of England*, Sutton, 1987.

73   ibid.

74   As quoted by Eric de Maré in *The Canals of England*.

75   'Partnership with the People', British Waterways, June 1999.

76   Fathers, *The Regent's Canal*.

77   Thomas De Quincey, *Confessions of an English Opium-Eater*, Dover, 1995. First published 1821.

78   Criminal broadside in the Museum of London's online collection available to view online at:
    http://collections.museumoflondon.org.uk/Online/object.aspx?objectID=object-447136&start=1&rows=1#.dpuf

79   Book illustration in the Museum of London's online collection available to view online at:

http://collections.museumoflondon.org.uk/Online/object.aspx?
objectID=object-795045&start=3&rows=1

80   Richard Henry Horne, 'Dust; Or, Ugliness Redeemed', *Household Words*, Vol. 1, 13 July 1850.
http://www.djo.org.uk/household-words/volume-i/page-379.html

'In July 1850, shortly after the removal of the Great Dustheap to make way for the building of King's Cross station (part of the newly commissioned Great Northern Railway), Richard Henry Horne published an article in Dickens's journal *Household Words*, titled "Dust; Or, Ugliness Redeemed". The piece merges documentary reportage of observed dust heaps with a retrospective description of the now absent "great Dust-heap" ... Horne's sympathetic account of the community of dust-sifters, as well as his suggestion of the dust heap as a repository for treasures and fortune, gives impetus to Dickens's novel more than a decade later.' – Heather Tilley, 'Ashes to Cashes: the Value of Dust', Dickens Our Mutual Friend Reading Project.
https://dickensourmutualfriend.wordpress.com/2014/07/17/ashes-to-cashes-the-value-of-dust/

81   Permanent exhibition, London Canal Museum.

82   'Partnership with the People', British Waterways.

83   The Inland Waterways Association was formed in 1946 to campaign for the greater use of the waterways and to resist the deterioration and frequent abandonment of the canals that was then taking place. Tom Rolt, author of *Narrowboat*, was one of the founders.
https://www.waterways.org.uk/waterways/history/history_

84   'Partnership with the People', British Waterways.

85   Daniel Johnson, 'Gasometers: a brief history', *Telegraph*, 26 November 2013.
http://www.telegraph.co.uk/finance/newsbysector/energy/oilandgas/10473071/Gasometers-a-brief-history.html

86   Tom Bateman, 'Does London need a £4.2bn "super-sewer"?' *BBC News*, 12 September 2013.
http://www.bbc.co.uk/news/uk-england-london-24046324

87   'London's "super sewer" gets the go ahead', *BBC News*, 12 September 2014.
http://www.bbc.co.uk/news/uk-england-london-29175607

88   One bedroom flat for sale at Grosvenor Waterside, advertised on Zoopla at £875,000, June 2015.

89   Virginia Woolf, *A Room of One's Own*, Penguin, 1945, first published 1929.

90   As quoted by Alan Hollinghurst in the introduction to the 2013 ebook edition of *Offshore*, published by Fourth Estate.

91   Paul Atterbury, 'Steam & Speed: Industry, Power & Social Change in 19th-Century Britain', Victoria and Albert Museum website.
     http://www.vam.ac.uk/content/articles/s/industry-power-and-social-change/

92   Mayor of London, 'Connecting with London's nature: The Mayor's Biodiversity Strategy', Greater London Authority, July 2002.
     http://legacy.london.gov.uk/mayor/strategies/biodiversity/docs/strat_full.pdf

93   'The Bats of London', London Bat Group website.
     http://www.londonbats.org.uk/lonbats.htm

94   As quoted by Richard J. King in *The Devil's Cormorant*, University of New Hampshire Press, 2014.

95   Cocker and Mabey, *Birds Britannica*.

96   ibid.

97   Ted Hughes, 'A Cormorant', *Three Books*, Faber and Faber, 1993.

98   Fathers, *The Regent's Canal*.

99   One bedroom, 547 square foot flat for sale at Merchant Square, advertised on Zoopla at £749,995, March 2015.

100   'Two new permanent trade moorings in Paddington', Canal and River Trust website, 14 November 2014.
     https://canalrivertrust.org.uk/news-and-views/news/two-new-permanent-trade-moorings-in-paddington
     'CaRT to close floating bookshop', *Narrowboat World*, 24 November 2014.
     http://www.narrowboatworld.com/index.php/news-flash/7500-cart-tp-close-floating-bookshop

101   The Work on Water website advertises a fleet of eighteen office barges for rent at Merchant Square/Paddington Basin,

explaining the developer is Paddington Basin Business Barges Ltd, which is 'a joint venture between the developers responsible for Paddington Basin – European Land and Property Ltd & Canal & River Trust'.

http://www.workonwater.com

102   London Assembly Environment Committee, 'Moor or less: Mooring on London's Waterways'.

103   J.G. Ballard writing in *London, City of Disappearances*, Hamish Hamilton, 2006.

104   Harry Wallop, 'London's "bread basket" wrestles to keep costs down as even foodies cut back', *Telegraph*, 18 February 2012.

http://www.telegraph.co.uk/finance/newsbysector/
retailandconsumer/9090329/Londons-bread-basket-wrestles-to
-keep-costs-down-as-even-foodies-cut-back.html

105   Cellulose acetate in the Museum of London's online collection available to view online at:

http://collections.museumoflondon.org.uk/Online/object.aspx?
objectID=object-910423&start=3&rows=1

106   Jim Shead, 'More than a mooring – Uxbridge Boat Centre'. First published in *Waterways World*, January 2004.

http://www.jim-shead.com/waterways/Articles.php?wpage=86

107   Tony Kushner, *Angels in America, Part One: Millennium Approaches*, Nick Hern Books, 1993.

108   'Old Oak Common plans approved by Eric Pickles', *BBC News*, 28 January 2015.

http://www.bbc.co.uk/news/uk-england-london-31019498

109   G.K. Chesterton, 'The Rolling English Road'.

Bibliography

Books

Ackroyd, Peter. *London the Biography.* Vintage, 2001.

Ackroyd, Peter. *London Under.* Chatto & Windus, 2011.

Ackroyd, Peter. *Thames, Sacred River.* Chatto & Windus, 2007.

Cocker, Mark and Richard Mabey. *Birds Britannica.* Chatto & Windus, 2005.

De Maré, Eric. *The Canals of England.* Sutton, 1987. First published 1950.

De Quincey, Thomas. *Confessions of an English Opium-Eater.* Dover Publications Inc., 1995. First published 1821.

Dickens, Charles. *Bleak House.* Penguin, 1994. First published 1852–3.

Dickens, Charles. *Night Walks.* Penguin, 2010. Taken from *Selected Journalism 1850–70.*

Fathers, David. *The Regent's Canal.* Frances Lincoln, 2012.

Fitter, R.S.R. *London's Birds.* Collins, 1949.

Fitter, R.S.R. *London's Natural History.* Collins, 1945.

Fitzgerald, Penelope. *Offshore.* Fourth Estate, 2013. First published 1979.

Goode, David. *Wild in London.* Michael Joseph, 1986.

Hadfield, Charles. *The Canals of South and South East England.* David & Charles, 1969.

Herbert, A.P. *The Water Gipsies.* House of Stratus, 2001. First published 1930.

Hudson, W.H. *Birds in London.* New Readers Library, 1928. First
    published 1898.

Jones, Barbara. *The Unsophisticated Arts.* Little Toller Books,
    2013. First published 1951.

King, Richard J. *The Devil's Cormorant.* University of New
    Hampshire Press, 2014.

Knowles, Michael. *Saving the Walthamstow Marshes.*
    Self-published, 2015.

Kushner, Tony. *Angels in America, Part One: Millennium
    Approaches.* Nick Hern Books, 1993.

Lessing, Doris. *The Golden Notebook.* Fourth Estate, 2013. First
    published 1962.

Mabey, Richard. *A Good Parcel of English Soil.* Penguin, 2013.

Mabey, Richard. *The Unofficial Countryside.* Little Toller Books,
    2010. First published 1973.

Moorcock, Michael. *Mother London.* Pocket Books, 2004. First
    published 1988.

Orwell, George. *The Road to Wigan Pier.* Penguin, 1972. First
    published 1937.

Pirsig, Robert. *Zen and the Art of Motorcycle Maintenance.*
    Vintage, 2004. First published 1974.

Purvis, Richard. *Lichens.* Natural History Museum, 2000.

Rolt, L.T.C. *Narrowboat.* The History Press, 2013. First
    published 1944.

Sinclair, Iain, ed. *London, City of Disappearances.* Hamish
    Hamilton, 2006.

Sinclair, Iain. *London Orbital.* Penguin, 2003.

Talling, Paul. *London's Lost Rivers.* Random House, 2011.

Winter, Kathleen. *Boundless.* Jonathan Cape, 2015.

Winterson, Jeanette. *Why Be Happy When You Could Be Normal?*
    Vintage, 2012.

Woolf, Virginia. *A Room of One's Own*. Penguin, 1945. First
    published 1929.
Woolfson, Esther. *Field Notes From a Hidden City*. Granta,
    2014.

Field Guides

Chinery, Michael. *Field Guide to the Wildlife of Britain and Europe*.
    Parragon, 1987.
Grey-Wilson, Christopher. *Eyewitness Handbooks Wild Flowers
    of Britain and Northwest Europe*. Dorling Kindersley,
    1995.
Harrap, Simon. *RSPB Pocket Guide to British Birds*. Helm,
    2007.
Hume, Rob. *RSPB Birds of Britain and Europe*. Dorling
    Kindersley, 2006.
Lippert, W. and D. Podlech. *Wildflowers of Britain & Europe*.
    Collins, 1994.
Wolseley, Pat and Holger Thüs. *The OPAL Guide to Common
    Lichens*. OPAL, 2013.

Poetry and Lyrics

Chesterton, G.K. 'The Rolling English Road'. (Poem of the
    Week. *Guardian*, 13 June 2011.)
Clampitt, Amy. 'The Cormorant in Its Element'. *The Devil's
    Cormorant*. University of New Hampshire Press, 2014.
Eliot, T.S. 'The Waste Land'. *Collected Poems 1909–1962*. Faber
    and Faber, 1977.
Hughes, Ted. 'A Cormorant'. *Three Books*. Faber and Faber, 1993.
Hughes, Ted. 'The Moorhen'. *Three Books*. Faber and Faber, 1993.
Milton, John. 'Paradise Lost'. *Complete Poems*. www.bartleby.
    com/4/401.html.

Selected Articles

Horne, Richard Henry. 'Dust; Or, Ugliness Redeemed'. *Household Words*. Vol. 1. 13 July 1850.

Meikle, James and Phil Maynard. 'Canal boats: the last option for affordable city-centre living?' *Guardian*, 11 November 2014.

Moore, Rowan. 'Britain's housing crisis is a human disaster. Here are 10 ways to solve it'. *Observer*, 15 March 2015.

Knight, David. 'Living on Infrastructure. Community and Conflict on the Canal Network'. *Critical Cities. Ideas, Knowledge and Agitation from Emerging Urbanists*. Vol. 2. 2010: 216–25.

Rosen, Jonathan. 'Because It's Ugly'. Review of *The Double-Crested Cormorant: Plight of a Feathered Pariah* by Linda Wires. *London Review of Books*. Vol. 36, No. 19. 9 October 2014.

Tushingham, David. 'I already have a golem, many of them. Interview with Paul Barritt'. Programme for *Golem* by 1927. Young Vic, 2014.

Film and Audio

The Barge Fellows, Studies on the Regent's Canal. British Pathé, 1926. Available in the British Pathé Archive, ID 894.25, and online at http://www.britishpathe.com/video/the-barge-fellows-studies-on-the-regents-canal-1

Regent's Canal. British Pathé, 1938. Available in the British Pathé Archive, ID 1256.26, and online at http://www.britishpathe.com/video/regents-canal

Corn by Canal. British Pathé, 1940. Available in the British Pathé Archive, ID 1204.26, and online at http://www.britishpathe.com/video/corn-by-canal

Bibliography

Venice in London. British Pathé, 1963. Available in the
    British Pathé Archive, ID 1756.03, and online at
    http://www.britishpathe.com/video/venice-in-london
Betjemen, John. *Metroland.* BBC, 1973. Available online at
    https://vimeo.com/89603339
Miller, Frank & Harry B. Parkinson. *Barging through London.*
    Graham-Wilcox Productions, 1924. Available online at
    https://m.youtube.com/watch?v=9hefWqfn668

Reports

Commission for a Sustainable London 2012. 'London 2012:
    From Vision to Reality'. November 2012.
Game, Meg and John Whitfield. 'Nature Conservation in Tower
    Hamlets. Ecology Handbook 27'. London Ecology Unit, 1996.
Lee Valley Regional Park Authority. 'Site Management Plan.
    2012–2017. Walthamstow Marshes'.
London Assembly Environment Committee. 'Moor or less:
    Mooring on London's Waterways'. Greater London
    Authority, November 2013.
London Biodiversity Partnership. 'Standing Water Habitat
    Action Plan'. 2008.
Mayor of London. 'Connecting with London's nature: The
    Mayor's Biodiversity Strategy'. Greater London Authority,
    July 2002.
Regent's Canal Group. 'The Regent's Canal – a policy for its
    future'. 1967.
Save the Marshes Campaign. 'Walthamstow Marshes: The
    1970s Survey'. 2007.
Smith, Chloe. 'An Ecological Search for London's Canals and
    the Lee Navigation on behalf of Helen Babbs'. Greenspace
    Information for Greater London, April 2015.

Stearn, Jacqui. 'The potential for wildlife habitats along the
    Regent's Canal in Camden'. London Wildlife Trust, 1983.
Waite, Michael, Daniel Keech and Meg Game. 'Nature
    Conservation in Camden. Ecology Handbook 24'. London
    Ecology Unit, 1993.

Acknowledgements

This book has been shaped and informed by some brilliant people. I would like to say a special thank you to Anna Luker Gilding and Lucy Anna Scott for their encouragement, constructive criticism and good advice; to my agent Josephine Hayes and my editor Kiera Jamison, and to Kate Hewson for the original commission; to Paul Barritt, John Bryden, Annie Chipchase, Ben Fenton, Mathew Frith, Rob Humphreys, Chloe Smith, Theo Thomas and Katelyn Toth Fejel for their time, generosity and knowledge; to Bell Lomax Moreton, Greenspace Information for Greater London, Icon Books, London Waterkeeper, London Wildlife Trust, Puppet Barge and Thames 21 for their help and support. And, most of all, I would like to thank S., for just being him.

— ◆◆◆ —

Adrift describes a ten-month period from January to October 2014 when I was living with my partner on our cruising canal boat in London. The east to west journey mapped out here is a simplified version of our travels over that time. Most of the text was written during the first half of 2015 and some of the articles I quote from were published that year. The changes to boat licensing for those without a home mooring outlined in chapter 10 were announced in early 2015; I have included them here as their impact could be significant. Facts, figures and web addresses were all correct at the time of going to print.

My intention with this book was to document some of the life – both wild and human, and including my own – that London's rivers and canals can and do support; to make an argument for their value, and as much more than mere wallpaper. It felt important to do this at a time when urban waterways' rough edges are being smoothed out, when London's alternative spaces are becoming increasingly corporate, and when the position of her live-aboard boaters – people who are often lazily belittled as hipsters or bums – seems especially precarious. I hope the perspective of someone living on the water will be interesting to others and that *Adrift* adds at least something new to the great many books that have already been written about London. This is very much a personal account and in no way represents the views of anyone other than myself, least of all other boaters.

Acknowledgements

By the time the book is published I will have been living on the water for almost three years, both as a continuous cruiser and more recently with a longer-term mooring; it continues to be glorious and incredibly hard work, every single day. There is still plenty to learn. If you are thinking of buying a boat to live on, please do your research first and don't make the decision lightly.

HB, 2016.